The Roaring of the
SACRED RIVER

The Wilderness Quest
for Vision and Self-Healing

STEVEN FOSTER
AND
MEREDITH LITTLE

Prentice Hall Press

New York   London   Toronto   Sydney   Tokyo

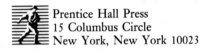 Prentice Hall Press
15 Columbus Circle
New York, New York 10023

PRENTICE HALL PRESS and colophon are registered trademarks of
Simon & Schuster, Inc.

Library of Congress Cataloging-in-Publication Data

Foster, Steven, 1936–
    The roaring of the sacred river : the wilderness quest for vision and
self-healing / Steven Foster and Meredith Little. — 1st ed.

    p. cm.
    Includes bibliographical references.
    ISBN 0-13-781445-3 : $9.95
    1. Spiritual life. 2. Rites and ceremonies. 3. Vision quests. 4. New
Age movement. 5. Wilderness (Theology) I. Little, Meredith,
1951– . II. Title.
BL624.F675 1989
291.3'8—dc20   89-37846
                                                                 CIP

Manufactured in the United States of America

10 9 8 7 6 5 4 3 2 1

First Edition

This Book is Dedicated to
Grandmother Ethel Twycross Foster
and
Grandmother Annabelle Bagley Hine

With hundreds of thousands and millions of units
We make wine and sweet spirits
And offer them to our ancestors . . .
Thus to fulfill all the rites,
And bring down blessings to all.
—from the Chinese *Book of Odes* (*circa* 1000 B.C.)

Acknowledgments

This book reveals our need to live fully the story of our life partnership, the plot of which involves the demonstration of our "vision on earth for the people to see." We could no more keep from writing this book than a plant can help drinking air and breathing water. But if our "people" had not existed, this book would not exist. Nurtured by their regard, encouragement, and instruction, we could not help but give away what was given to us.

Virginia Hine (now deceased), our anthropological consultant and grandmother, once took the vision quest name of "Gift Bearer." "I don't want to be the big cheese who gives the gift," she explained. "I want to be the little page in the fancy dress who carries the gift on a velvet pillow. I want to be the *bearer* of the gift." Our sentiments exactly. We will be quite happy to place the gift in the receiver's hands.

We have received contributions of inestimable worth from others. What they gave brightened and enriched the gift we are bearing. We are pleased to share the velvet pillow with them. Thank you, Virginia Hine, for consenting to be our "spirit guide," for all the teaching you imparted (and still impart) to us, and for your cheerful, ready, sensible support throughout the writing of this book. Thank you Hyemeyohsts Storm (né Dust Devil), for the motive genius of your teaching, for your crafty yarns, for your version of Jumping Mouse, Frog, and the Sacred River, and for instruction in the four directions and shields. As time passes, the genius of your mixed-blood mythopoeia will help resolve the American cultural predicament.

Traditional, nontraditional, and Métis teachers and medicine people have a hand in this book. Thank you Sun Bear, Wabun, Shawnodese, and Robert Greenway. Thank you, Dire Wolf,

Rocky, Stephanie, and Swiftdeer. Thank you Evelyn Eaton, Brooke Medicine Eagle, and Edie Newcomb. Thank you, Tom Pinkson, Brant Secunda, Bill Bridges, Tom Brown, Dennis Banks, and Link Sees Two Bears. Thank you, Rolling Thunder on the Mountain, for validation given years ago.

Without the Raccoons listed below, much of the subject matter would not exist. In the breast of the book beat their combined Métis hearts. Thank you, Jack Crimmins, Jennifer, Drew Pratt, Marilyn Riley, Ron Pevney, Linda Gregory, Sunwater, Adele Getty, Beau Leonhart, John Morris, and others. Now we must inherit the consequences of what we created together.

Without the friendship, financial aid, consultation, and support of certain angels, we would not have been able to go on. These also lend a hand in bearing the gift. Thank you Phil and Elizabeth Little, Marilyn Mountain, Tim Garthwaite, Howard and Sue Lamb, Howard and Jan Voskuyl, Mike Groza, Jonathan Swift-Turttle, Steve Blair, Pat Nalley, Mike Riley, E.M.T., Frank Burton, Natalie Rogers, Carmen Bier, and Edward Beggs.

We want to mention all those "Mice" whose experience and journal entries forever reside now in the pages of this book. Thank you for teaching us lessons that we will never forget; thank you for hallowing Grandmother Nature and the vision fast with your lives.

To our parents, stepparents, children, and stepchildren we also want to express our love and respect. For the lessons of parenthood and childhood, for unconditional love poured out of us and through us, thank you, Elizabeth, Phil, Ginny, Aldie, Warren, Winifred, Kevin, Shelley, Keenan, Patricia, Christian, and Selene.

Contents

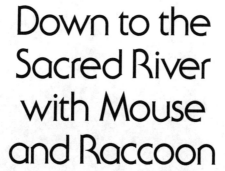

INTRODUCTION

Down to the Sacred River with Mouse and Raccoon

We will begin with the first half of a classic retelling of an old American Indian fable, "Jumping Mouse":

Once there was a Mouse.

He was a Busy Mouse, Searching Everywhere, Touching his Whiskers to the Grass, and Looking. He was Busy as all Mice are, Busy with Mice things. But Once in a while he would Hear an odd Sound. He would Lift his Head, Squinting hard to See, his Whiskers Wiggling in the Air, and he would Wonder. One day he Scurried up to a fellow Mouse and asked him, "Do you Hear a Roaring in your Ears, my Brother?"

"No, no," answered the Other Mouse, not Lifting his Busy Nose from the Ground. "I Hear Nothing. I am Busy now. Talk to me Later."

He asked Another Mouse the same Question and the Mouse Looked at him Strangely. "Are you Foolish in your Head? What Sound?" he asked and Slipped into a Hole in a Fallen Cottonwood Tree.

The little Mouse shrugged his Whiskers and Busied himself again, Determined to Forget the Whole Matter. But there was that Roaring again. It was faint, very faint, but it was there! One Day, he Decided to investigate the Sound just a little. Leaving the Other Busy Mice, he Scurried a little Way away and Listened again. There it was! He was Listening hard when suddenly, Someone said Hello.

"Hello, little Brother," the Voice said, and Mouse almost jumped right Out of his Skin. He Arched his Back and Tail and was about to Run.

"Hello," again said the Voice. "It is I, Brother Raccoon." And sure enough, It was! "What are you Doing Here all by yourself, little Brother?" asked the Raccoon. The Mouse blushed and put his nose almost to the Ground. "I Hear a Roaring in my Ears and I am Investigating it," he answered timidly.

"A Roaring in your Ears?" replied the Raccoon as he Sat Down with him. "What you Hear, little Brother, is the River."

"The River?" Mouse asked curiously. "What is a River?"

"Walk with me and I will Show you the River," Raccoon said.

Little Mouse was terribly Afraid, but he was Determined to Find Out Once and for All about the Roaring. "I can Return to my Work," he thought, "after this thing is Settled, and possibly this thing may Aid me in All my Busy Examining and Collecting. And my Brothers All said it was Nothing. I will Show them. I will Ask Raccoon to Return me and I will have Proof."

"All right Raccoon, my Brother," said Mouse. "Lead on to the River. I will Walk with you."

Little Mouse Walked with Raccoon. His little Heart was Pounding in his Breast. The Raccoon was Taking him upon Strange Paths and little Mouse Smelled the Scent of many things that had Gone by this Way. Many times he became so Frightened he almost Turned Back. Finally, they Came to the River! It was Huge and Breathtaking, Deep and Clear in Places, and Murky in Others. Little Mouse was unable to See Across it because it was so Great. It Roared, Sang, Cried, and Thundered on its Course. Little Mouse Saw Great and Little Pieces of the World Carried Along on its Surface.

"It is Powerful!" little Mouse said, Fumbling for Words.

"It is a Great thing," answered the Raccoon, "but here, let me Introduce you to a Friend."

In a Smoother, Shallower Place was a Lily Pad, Bright and Green. Sitting upon it was a Frog, almost as Green as the Pad it sat on. The Frog's White Belly stood out Clearly.

"Hello, little Brother," said the Frog. "Welcome to the River."

"I must Leave you Now," cut in Raccoon, "but do not Fear, little Brother, for Frog will Care for you Now." And Raccoon Left, Looking along the River Bank for Food that he might Wash and Eat.

Little Mouse Approached the Water and Looked into it. He saw a Frightened Mouse Reflected there.

"Who are you?" little Mouse asked the Reflection. "Are you Afraid being that Far out into the Great River?"

"No," answered the Frog, "I am not Afraid. I have been Given the Gift from Birth to Live both Above and Within the River. When Winter Man Comes and Freezes this Medicine, I cannot be Seen. But all the while Thunderbird Flies, I am here. To Visit me, One must Come when the World is Green. I, my Brother, am the Keeper of the Water."

"Amazing!" little Mouse said at last, again Fumbling for Words.

"Would you like to have some Medicine power?" Frog asked.

4

"Medicine Power? Me?" asked little Mouse. "Yes, yes! If it is Possible."

"Then Crouch as Low as you Can, and then Jump as high as you are Able! You will have your Medicine!" Frog said.

Little Mouse did as he was Instructed. He Crouched as Low as he Could and Jumped. And when he did, his Eyes Saw the Sacred Mountains.

Little Mouse could hardly Believe his Eyes. But there They were! But then he Fell back to Earth, and he Landed in the River!

Little Mouse became Frightened and Scrambled back to the Bank. He was Wet and Frightened nearly to Death.

"You have Tricked me," little Mouse Screamed at the Frog!

"Wait," said the Frog. "You are not Harmed. Do not let your Fear and Anger Blind you. What did you See?"

"I," Mouse stammered, "I, I Saw the Sacred Mountains!"

"And you have a New Name!" Frog said. "It is Jumping Mouse."

"Thank you, Thank you," Jumping Mouse said, and Thanked him again. "I want to Return to my People and Tell them of this thing that has Happened to me. . . ."

—Hyemeyohsts Storm, *Seven Arrows* [1]

The story continues. Jumping Mouse returns to his people, but they view him with fear and disbelief. Nevertheless, he cannot forget his vision of the Sacred Mountains. Finally, in fear and trembling, he sets out on a journey to find them. Many adventures befall him. These will be discussed later in the book. Suffice it to say that Jumping Mouse is a good story to tell people. It makes them laugh and cry at the same time. They identify with little Mouse. They too hear a roaring in their ears—and want to investigate. They too want to jump as high as they are able and see the Sacred Mountains shining in the distance.

Although Mouse is by far the most frequently mentioned character, Raccoon is the real subject of this book, whose subtitle might be: "A Training Manual for Raccoons Who Want to Take Mouse Down to the Sacred River." That is why we are interested in whether or not you are "Raccoon"—for Raccoon is Raccoon, no matter what else he is. You could be a teacher, counselor, parent, grandparent, aunt, uncle, minister, priest, wilderness guide, psychologist, doctor, housewife, house husband, medicine chief, or general factotum, but there is an essential part of you that recognizes the benefit of taking Mouse down to the Sacred River. However you came by this precious understanding, we invite your continued attention.

Note that Raccoon did not try to "doctor" Mouse—that is, diagnose the problem as "roaring disease" and prescribe a pill to alleviate the symptoms—nor did he try to psychoanalyze Mouse, save his soul, or sell him anything. All he said was, "Walk with me and I will Show you the River." He did not use fancy words to describe the mysterious Sacred River. In fact, he hardly said anything at all about it until they got there. Then he remarked simply, "It is a Great thing." Of course he could see that little Mouse was in deep distress and in the throes of giving birth to himself. But he did not put in his two cents to say what was ailing Mouse. He did not manipulate Mouse into thinking or believing this or that about his so-called problem. His role was to serve Mouse, to take him down to the source of the roaring and to introduce him to the "Keeper of the Waters." Having accomplished his task, he did not even stick around to cheer Jumping Mouse on. He vanished into the cover along the river, looking for "Food that he might Wash and Eat."

In the tale, Raccoon plays a "maieutic" role in Mouse's life. Webster's defines *maieutic* as: "Designating or of the Socratic method of helping a person to bring forth and become aware of his latent ideas, gifts, or memories." "Bring forth" is a key phrase. Raccoon helped Mouse bring himself forth. Socrates' admonition, "Know thyself," does not mean that all students' questions are answered for them. Socrates meant that with the aid of a teacher, students could arrive at the answers on their own. This bringing forth from within of self-knowledge is a kind of birthing process. When Raccoon, the "midwife," saw that Mouse was almost "at term," he performed his role as intermediary. He took Mouse down to the Sacred River and introduced him to Frog. There Mouse gave birth to Jumping Mouse. The British philosopher Charles Bennet describes this midwifely function as being "like the man in Plato's Allegory of the Cave who knew that his chief task was to turn the prisoners around so that they could face in the direction of the sun. The sun would do the rest."[2]

Yes, Raccoon knew what the roaring was all about. He knew he could not describe it. Mouse needed direct experience of *it*. Without this direct experience he would have remained like the other Mice—afraid of knowing and afraid of not knowing. He would never have returned from the Sacred River wet and glistening with this new thing he knew about himself. He would never have seen that his life held a greater destiny than a comfortable nest in Mouseland.

Raccoon guided Mouse through a rite of passage. The principal players in the questing rite are Mouse, Raccoon, and Frog. Because Raccoon knows that any association with Frog (and the Sacred River of which he is Keeper) is good for Mouse, he acts as the agent of Frog. Who is Frog? Frog is symbolic of Mother Nature herself, in all her manifestations in the sky, in all the creatures and growing things who are our sisters and brothers. His "medicine advice" to little Mouse is the very essence of a questing ceremony: "Crouch as Low as you Can, and then Jump as High as you are Able! You will have your Medicine!"

Modern wilderness passage rites—in which Raccoon assumes a role similar to his counterpart in the fable—are complex in detail but essentially as simple in meaning as this tale. Mouse is an individual (aged twelve to eighty) of either sex or sexual preference, usually of mixed ethnic heritage and tradition, from any walk of life, professing any creed or value system, often in the throes of a life crisis, or passing from one life stage to the next. For one reason or another—is it the roaring in his ears?—he seeks to birth his spirit from the constricted circle of his own self-imposed limitations by electing to participate in the quest. That is when he bumps into Raccoon.*

Raccoon is an individual, regardless of sex or sexual preference, ethnic heritage or creed, from any walk of life, who helps Mouse prepare to leave Mouseland and the past behind. He conducts Mouse safely down to the Sacred River and introduces him to the spirit of Mother Nature. Raccoon then leaves Mouse behind while Mouse lives alone for a period of time, often without food, sometimes without water, beside the Sacred River, listening to the clear advice of brother Frog. During the time modern Mouse is alone,

*The use of masculine pronouns throughout this book is solely for grammatical consistency. The feminine is always implied.

7

Raccoon lurks nearby, ready to be of aid if Mouse gets into trouble. When the time comes for Jumping Mouse (formerly Mouse) to leave the Sacred River and go back to his people, Raccoon helps him get ready to go back to Mouseland to start out on his new life.

In modern rites, as in the fable, the Sacred River plays an all-important part in the drama of transformation. The Sacred River is the wilderness place, the hallowed ground set apart, the mountain top, the canyon, the grove of trees, the spring, the hole dug in the earth, the cave, or the crudely built lodge in the forest outside town. The Sacred River is a place of power, a consecrated arena, a natural womb in which vision is conceived. Animated by the spirit of nature, the Sacred River "roars, sings, cries, and thunders on its course." The Sacred River is our true home. When Mouse goes there he is really going home to his true Mother—the Mother to whom he will finally yield his life.

Traditional rite-of-passage ceremonies, such as the practice of fasting alone in the wilderness for vision, tend to weaken in the face of advancing civilization, but they do not die. Like seeds, these ceremonies lie dormant in the dark, rich soil of the unconscious. Generations may pass before they are renewed by the sun and rain of creative human insight. When the ancient practices are revived, the sacred ancestors awaken, too, and begin to whisper again. The whispering increases to a roar—the roaring of the Sacred River.

At the present time, organizations concerned with rites of passage are springing up throughout the country. Individuals are being trained as Raccoons. Here and there, high schools, colleges, and other institutions are including the vision fast in their curricula, programs, or methodology. In increasing numbers Mice are coming out of their holes, sniffing the air, convinced they hear a roaring in their ears. Are there enough Raccoons around for them to bump into?

The concepts, symbols, allegories, and teachings described in this book evolved from four years of weekly training sessions at Rites of Passage, Inc. (Northern California), a nonprofit vision-quest organization (for youth and adults) which we codirected for several years. We called these weekly meetings "Raccoon Lodge." Over a period of time, many Raccoons of diverse ethnic backgrounds showed up for these meetings. None of us could lay claim to "pure blood." Born and raised in America, we embodied the

Métis, or ethnically mixed culture, that America is gradually becoming. We called ourselves "native Americans," as distinguished from "native American Indians," the original inhabitants of this land. Month after month, our attentions were absorbed by the many traditions and teachings of wilderness rites of passage. By the miraculous processes of synthesis and integration, all the different ethnic colors were blended into a rainbow whole. As you will notice, the allegories and ceremonies described in these pages owe their existence to widely divergent ethnic or cultural sources.

Consider the mixed ancestry of the Raccoon. Note the color of his coat. His mama must have been white and his daddy must have been black. But see how the blacks and whites blend into the greys, browns and reds. What color are his eyes? He must have some yellow in his genes as well. Surely, this fellow cannot be a product of inbreeding. He is so omnivorous, so adaptable. How adroitly he pries the lids off garbage cans, regardless of their owners! How easily he moves through the darkness between the mansion and the ghetto, the jungle and the desert, the wilderness and the world of civilization! It must be that many different sacred ancestors counsel him.

Seventeen years ago, we were first introduced to the Sacred River ceremony by a Raccoon who took us to the source of the roaring in our ears. Our noses had been pressed up to the ground for so long that we hardly recognized the amplitude and power of what we heard. But Grandmother Earth took pity on our near-sightedness. She listened to our naive prayers and fastened them to the silent stars. She introduced us to Lizard, Snake, Coyote, and Canyon Wren—alias "Frog." They gave us the courage to jump as high as we were able. We jumped. What did it matter that we landed in a thicket of prickly pear? We had seen the Sacred Mountains! We returned to our people, filled with excitement to tell them what we had seen. That was when the vision quest of our lives began.

The time has come to bring wilderness life-passage ceremonies into the open, up from the "forgotten works" of human culture. For too long they have been shrouded in ignorance, prejudice, misinformation, and fear—nor is there any need to be bashful about exhibiting the *sacra* for public inspection. There is nothing to hide. These ceremonies are what they are: private knowings in each

Mouse who goes down to the Sacred River, looks into the mirror of the waters, and hears the voice of Frog. These ceremonies "belong" to no one—unless it be Mouse. There are some who say: "What you do is a sacrilege. By making these things public you cheapen them, soil them. Don't you realize what man does with everything he touches?"

> And all is smeared with trade; bleared, smeared with toil;
> And wears man's smudge and shares man's smell:
> . . . nor can foot feel, being shod.
> —G. M. Hopkins, "God's Grandeur"

How can we deny that humans profane what they touch? Even the act of putting these ideas into words between the pages of a book can be seen as a cheapening of ancient truths. But inner imperatives insist that the truth will out. We are but the channels, the "cracked and earthen vessels" leaking so badly we could hardly contain the fullness poured into us long enough to finish this book. Many times we have gone into the desert to ask if it was right or good for us to speak of these things. Many spirits replied—the stones of the desert pavement, ripped up by the passing of ORVs, the bristlecone stump, severed to make tourist souvenirs, the gopher snake, smashed but still twitching on the newly paved road through the National Forest, the buzzard-eaten carcass of a coyote tricked by poisoned bait. They all answered "Yes!" As one, they called to us: "Get back to your work! There is much to do!"

The heroes and heroines of this book are Mouse and Raccoon. Buffalo, Wolf, and Eagle also figure prominently, but they will make their appearance at the end. The settings are Mouseland, the Sacred River, and the trail that sooner or later leads everyone to the Sacred Mountains. The name of the drama is "Fasting Alone in the Wilderness." The theater is Grandmother Earth, in all her manifestations, human or otherwise. The authors are a couple of scraggly Raccoons who finally assembled the contents of myriad garbage pails into a coherent sculpture.

Mouse, Raccoon, and Frog invite your attention. They seek to live in your imagination and to become part of the reality of your purpose. We want to make it very clear from the start that the name, "Mouse," is not a demeaning or derogatory term. It is a term of respect and endearment. Mouse is a symbol of the innocence and unknowing that lives inside us, that makes us so human, so vulnerable. This very creature is the one who hears the roaring of the Sacred River, who has the courage to leave his brothers and sisters behind and to enter the passage that leads from the end to the beginning. His is a great heart, a great spirit.

In the same vein, you must not take Raccoon for a bandit, just because he wears that mask over his eyes. His suspicious habit of snooping around in the dark also has no bearing on his true nature, which is good-hearted and altruistic. All in all, he is a pleasant companion to walk with on the way to the Sacred River. What crises led him to Raccoonhood? Every Raccoon has his own story. Ask one or two. They may tell you. Ask yourself: "Am I a Raccoon?"

First and last, and never least, comes Frog, sitting on a lily pad in the Sacred River. He's the culprit. He told us to jump as high as we were able. In this valley where we live, at the edge of the Great Basin desert, the Sacred River is very much in evidence. Frog calls in the chill hours of a winter morning—in the howl of a coyote. Frog walks in the upland Sierra meadows—in the form of a deer. Frog soars above the cottonwoods down by the river—on the wings of a red-shouldered hawk. Frog sings in the silence of the starry summer night—in the love call of the crickets. Frog whispers in the wings of the great horned owl, drones in the swarming of wild bees. Everywhere we go, Frog is there, asking us if we want "some Medicine power." All the while, the Sacred River roars, pulling us back into the onrush of night, down into the great sea from which we emerged. This book is Frog-talk. And all the credit goes to Frog. When we jumped as high as we were able, this book is what we saw.

—Steven Foster and Meredith Little
The School of Lost Borders
Inyo Co., CA
May, 1988

1

Modern
Wilderness
Passage
Rites

I suspect it was . . . the old story of the implacable
necessity of a man having honour within his own
natural spirit. A man cannot live and temper his
metal without honour. There is deep in him a sense of
heroic quest; and our modern way of life, with its
emphasis on security, its distrust of the unknown and
its elevation of abstract collective values has repressed
the heroic impulse to a degree that may produce the
most dangerous consequences.

—Laurens van der Post, *The Heart of the Hunter*

Human growth is characterized by conscious change. We must
pass from one life stage to the next. The mother-breast of infancy
atrophies when we are weaned. Weaning brings us into the world
of childhood. We pass from childhood into adolescence. Adulthood
looms ahead, a seemingly impassable barrier. One way or another
we become "adult," in society's eyes or in our own. We leave the
single state when we marry or enter a committed relationship.
Sometimes, we divorce, and reenter the single state at a later stage
of growth. We make our way through the various passages of our
middle age and later years, facing predictable crises brought about
by parenthood, aging, retirement, and death. Finally, we cross the
threshold and begin our sacred journey through the underworld of
death.

In traditional cultures, changes in life station were celebrated by
rites or ceremonies of passage. Everyone participated in these ceremonies. If they did not, they did not gain entrance to the next stage
of their lives. Without rites of passage, individuals could not have
understood their life transitions, nor could they have been capable
of assuming the social responsibilities and privileges required by
their change in life station. Without orderly rites of passage, tribal
units would have become unstable and ceased to survive.

In modern times, the rise of technological science, the emergence
of large nations and cities, the influence and omnipotence of the

media, the thickening of the walls between humans and their natural environment, the dawn of the computer age, the threat of thermonuclear annihilation, the breakdown of the basic family social unit, the dehumanizing pressure of modern life, and many other factors, have contributed to the weakening of traditional values, including the various ceremonies of life passage. The careful, ritual footprints left by our ancestors have been paved over by the traffic of modern civilization. As these changes have tended to drain contemporary life of meaningful spiritual or mythical content, the "old ways" are glaringly apparent by their absence.

Consider, for example, the modern rites of passage from childhood to adulthood. On the long awaited day, while their loved ones look on, graduating high school seniors march to solemn music. They find their place in rows and hear speeches made by school, civic, and student leaders. A religious official gives an interdenominational prayer. The students stand poised at the brink of adulthood, the childhood world of high school already receding into the past. As the music swells triumphantly, the graduates switch their tassels to the other side of their mortarboards.

Where is the experiential "ordeal of passage" by which they have demonstrated their worthiness to assume the mantle of maturity? The vision fast alone on the sacred mountain has devolved into the switching of a tassel. What high school graduate would claim that commencement "exercises" are adequate, meaningful, "experienced" proof that he is ready to begin an adult life?

A similar fate has befallen other life transitions, although there are heartening changes in certain areas such as childbirth, death, and dying. Separation and divorce, modern life transitions of great significance, are hardly celebrated at all, except in a lawyer's office or a court of law. The transition into middle age, according to the commercial media, is almost a disgrace, and certainly a misfortune. The predictable crises of middle age are not formalized into meaningful rites. Likewise, retirement is rarely marked by meaningful ceremony. We put the elderly "out to pasture" instead of celebrating their incorporation into community service as elders.

Other crises, such as death of a loved one, natural or unnatural accident, drug or alcohol addiction, physical or psychological illness, change of vocation or home, abortion, miscarriage, and many more, are not attended by social rites (outside the church) that enable the individual experientially (and symbolically) to pass through, comprehend, and put an end to, the crisis. Many question the ability of the church to perform culturally adequate rites of passage among its constituents given the fact that many of its symbols require modern reinterpretation.

Because our culture only dimly recognizes the value of traditional rites of passage, large numbers of us suffer changes in life status like victims—a burden to ourselves and others. Lacking inner resources garnered from a meaningful life, we all too often nurture negative pictures of ourselves as helpless pawns in the grimy paws of fate. We think someone else must heal us because we cannot heal ourselves. Someone else must lead us because we cannot lead ourselves. Someone else must be the hero or heroine for us because our lives are so narrow, so mundane, so predictable. What can we do? Our hands are tied, we are but the helpless victims of meaningless life stories.

How then does our culture deal with those who are in crisis, the symptoms of which we see everywhere? Panic, hysteria, shock, anxiety, uncertainty, anger, violence, boredom, apathy, drug abuse, apprehension, guilt, self-hatred, perversion, helplessness, and "psychosomatic illnesses" of all kinds stalk the streets of our cities and counties, demanding to be dealt with somehow. How *do* we deal with them? Do we offer services that enable us to resolve our own crises? Or do we offer services that enable individuals to go to experts (doctors, lawyers, ministers, psychiatrists, counselors, mediums, psychics, etc.) who resolve our problems for us?

Our churches offer services that enable people to resolve their own conflicts through participation in rites of confirmation, passage, or transformation. Although these rites are usually devoid of existential content, they are sufficient for some. But what of those who do not have a personal or religious myth or value system? They fish in troubled waters, unable to turn away from the past. All too easily they trap themselves in nets of their own making, or are snared by the tricks of predators. Either way, they are at risk to themselves, others, and the earth they live on. Can they be helped to see that they are not victims, that they possess the inner gumption to make sense of their quandary, that they *do* have a life story?

If you do not get it from yourself,
Where will you go for it?
          —*The Zenrin*

Therapeutic Problems
and How Mouse Solved His

Most therapeutic services provided by our culture exist to solve a
"problem" for "clients" or "patients." There is a tacit agreement
between therapist and patient that a problem exists, that the patient
cannot solve the problem himself, that therefore the patient has
come to the expert for a solution. Thus the patient surrenders his
ability to resolve his own issue and gives it to the medicine man,
therapist, reverend, doctor, or guru.

The expert, on his part, must center his attention on the problem,
attempting, of course, to see how the problem might be related to
other problems, complexes, or symptoms. He must review all the
ways of dealing with this problem and then come up with a solution, prescription, or treatment plan, a means of proceeding
whereby the problem is solved, alleviated, healed, or rendered in-
nocuous.

The traditional therapist must probe and watch, question and
listen, peeling away layers of symptomatic ideation, emotion, pro-
jection, introjection, or neurosis, like onion skin, moving ever
closer, hopefully, to the center of the problem. If all goes well, with
the cooperation of the client, the crisis will be resolved, and the
client become strong enough to walk on his own two feet. He will
not become further discouraged at his own inability to resolve the
crisis; he will not become dependent on the therapist; he will not
decide to change therapists.

It is not our intention to review the strengths and weaknesses of
problem-centered therapy. Its methodology is various and diverse.
The measure of its success is relative to the client, the therapist, and
the kind of therapy being practiced. There are "cures," "failures,"
and a wide range of outcomes. A great deal of time and energy is
expended for the purposes of solving the problem. To an extent,
society at large benefits from the problem's solution. The patient
resumes a "normal" or "productive" life. The therapist gets enough

money to continue his practice. More problems come to knock at his door. If he is good at what he does, he will soon become overwhelmed by people with problems.

Perhaps the best way to define how passage rites differ from problem-centered therapeutics is to go back to the Jumping Mouse story. Little Mouse was in the midst of a life crisis. He had a problem—a roaring in his ears. He went in search of a solution to his problem—and met Raccoon. If Raccoon had been a psychotherapist, he would have led Mouse to his office every week and talked about his problem. In time, perhaps, the roaring in Mouse's ears would have subsided. He would have returned to Mouseland and lived with the other mice, his hearing restored, once again a normal, productive member of Mouse society.

But Raccoon was not a psychiatrist. He was a "midwife" in a wilderness passage rite. He might have thought to himself, "Well, this little Mouse has a problem," but he did not say, "Stay with me, brother Mouse, and I will solve your problem." Instead, he said, "Walk with me and I will show you the River." Then Raccoon did a seemingly unforgivable thing. He left the little Mouse all alone with his problem. Surely he could see that his little brother was scared half to death. Why did he leave his "patient" alone to fend for himself? Fine problem-solver he turned out to be!

Raccoon, however, knew what he was doing. He knew that if Mouse were left alone in the midst of Mother Nature with the sound of roaring in his ears, he would come around to solving his own problem. He knew it wasn't a psychiatrist Mouse was looking for, but himself, reflected in the mirror of nature. He didn't even treat Mouse as though he had a problem. Instead, he introduced his friend to Frog, and went on his merry way.

Frog, as emissary of Mother Nature, didn't treat Mouse as though he had a problem either. He asked Mouse if he wanted some medicine. When the little fellow said yes, Frog told him to jump as high as he was able. He didn't ask Mouse to talk about the roaring in his ears. He told him to jump. When Mouse jumped, he resolved his problem. Of course, the cure didn't exactly help Jumping Mouse to live a normal life. But that is a story to tell in the last chapter.

The fact is, wilderness rites of passage are not problem-centered; they do not operate according to the theory that the "client's" problem must be solved. Traditional rites of passage adhere to the theory that the social imbalance caused by the crisis must be righted.[1] Undergoing the rite, initiation, or passage celebration, the "client" ends the problem, and the life crisis from whence it sprang, by virtue of his incorporation into a new life status. Rites of passage then, are community-centered. Benefit accrues to the community. Of course, there is added benefit to the "client," who has, via his existential passage, resolved the problem.

Although passage rites were not specifically designed to operate in a problem-oriented, therapeutic sense, they are rich with therapeutic metaphors, concepts, and methods. They are highly effective as means of accepting and finding meaning in life changes; of empowering individuals to be vital forces in the community; of engendering self-reliance, courage, endurance, and self-control; of activating self-healing mechanisms; of catalyzing personal encounters with the collective, archetypal unconscious; of igniting insight, wisdom, and illumination. Above all, they are designed to benefit the community at large. Not only does the "client" return to take his place as a member of society, but he returns with something even more powerful and rewarding to those around him, with what the ancients called "vision."

Therapeutic Implications
of Wilderness Passage Rites

Ancient psychological theory, of which wilderness passage rites are a part, regards life crisis or transition as challenges or opportunities of the highest order. As in mythical accounts of heroes and heroines, the quester dares much for stakes as high as the future of the human race. If he can encounter and "pass through" the dragon-ridden passage of personal crisis, he will emerge enlarged and renewed on the other side, where his community awaits his healing return.[2] The monomythic archetype of the questing hero or heroine runs deeply through the psychological experience of the passage rite, informing action, reflection and feeling.

Invariably, the heroic passage archetype is a story told in three parts or phases.[3] These phases are: end, middle, beginning; that is to say, the story begins with an ending and ends with a beginning:

> To make an end is to make a beginning.
> The end is where we start from.
> —T. S. Eliot, "Little Gidding"

Severance

Social anthropology calls the first phase *severance* or *separation*. The hero must leave everything behind, be cut off from the familiar past, removed from the civilized mother, weaned from everything outside himself that has sustained, defined, or inhibited him. Even as Jumping Mouse left the safe confines of Mouseland, so the quester turns his back on home, family, work, loved ones, and all modern conveniences.

But the hero can't simply walk away from it all. He must prepare. Sometimes he spends years in preparation, listening to the roaring in his ears, getting ready to make a big change in his life. As the time to make the change approaches, his commitment to the change is countered by his fear of the unknown. The deadline looms. He can no longer avoid the cutoff point, beyond which he cannot see. Yet he must prepare. Fear turns the butterflies in his belly into bats. Emotions and feelings well up even as he obeys the need to set his life in order, to rid himself of excess baggage, to savor his last moments, to review his past, even to ask forgiveness of those he might have wronged. Psychosomatic symptoms often arise, defensive shields freeze in the up position; feelings of vulnerability and defenselessness appear; unconscious material, long suppressed, comes to light; dreams often shift to the shadow side.

The modern therapist might find grist for the mill in the severance phase of the life passage story. When faced with the prospect of having to sever, the "client" and his "problem" grow together into one ball of anxiety and concern. As the deadline nears, the client cannot hide who he is. He stands naked, true to himself. "Why am I doing this?" he asks himself. "Am I really that ready to fast alone for four days and nights to celebrate the change in my life? Have I really come to the end of the old way?" His fears of the next phase of the story drive him deeper into himself, his relationships, his life, his commitment to change. Thus he becomes absorbed in the process of preparing to resolve his crisis.

Threshold

The second or middle phase of the passage rite story is called threshold, *limen* (Latin for "threshold"), or *marge* (French for "margin"). It comprises the adventure or ordeal of the hero, experienced within a sacred or consecrated natural place.[4] Raccoon left little Mouse alone at the Sacred River, at the threshold, the vestibule, the entryway to the vast mansion of nature, where the great, wild river ran unchecked and Frogs talked.

The root of the modern English term, threshold, is the Old English verb, *therscan*, "to thresh" or "thrash." The hero has come to the place where the wheat is threshed from the chaff, the grain thrashed from the corn. He will lose some of himself here. What is no longer important will fall away. One of the "boundary conditions" of a safe passage through this zone of magnified power will be the toll paid by his ego. If he has a "problem," the cost will be having to live alone with his problem in the sacred threshing-hold.

Combined with all the connotations of threshold (limit or limitation, border or borderland, margin or shore, cross or crossing, door or doorsill, opening or entrance) is the idea of passage. The hero passes through this threshold aperture, a fetal spirit negotiating the bardos of the underworld. Without food, shelter, or companionship, he must submit to the whims and wiles of his true Mother, to her rhythms of light and darkness, harsh and soft, growth and decay. In this intensely physical threshing-world there is a symbolic dimension, mirrored by everything he encounters. By the light of consciousness, images and reflections stand out in the natural mirror. Signs, clues, and deadly dragons mark his path. He is depressed, illumined, bored. He walks; he waits. Gradually he begins to birth himself.

The threshold, then, begins with a death, a severance, a dislocation. And then there is a passing through the sacred threshing-hold towards birth. This is the formula for human transformation.

From a therapist-client perspective, the threshold phase is full of potentially healing emotional states and therapeutic information.

Consider the evocative power of fasting, of isolation and loneliness, of exposure to the mysteries and omnipotent rhythms of Mother Nature. Consider the power of boredom to open doors of awareness, the power of weakness to find sources of strength, the power of loneliness to evoke those who are truly loved, the power of earth to teach centeredness, balance, and a sense of harmony with all things, the power of an approaching storm to ignite sensations of existential panic, the power of emptiness to produce feelings of fullness, the power of darkness to engender illumination, the power of light to cast shadow. These and many more would be at the therapist's touch could he but accompany the client into the threshold world.

In a way, the client-hero therapizes himself. Since he can't run away from himself, he has to accommodate his own behavior and its consequences, to make an order to his perception of things, to accept and "make sense" of himself. The very dust of the earth and the sweat of his body must be part of this resolution. The world of crisis left behind becomes an assimilated episode in his continuing life story. He celebrates the past with his own kind of ceremony, symbolically rendering it harmless. His witnesses are those he calls (in spirit) to attend his actions. Because he is alone, everything he does is for his (and their) eyes. Shielded from mortal sight, he can only be who he is, with a matchless opportunity to accept who he is. With the aid of nature, he resolves his story into an identity and a place on the earth, naked of pretense or illusion. In the mirror of nature he sees a name, a dream, a boon, a way to go ahead, an idea, a guidepost, a beacon, a knowing, a vision, another chapter in his life myth.

Incorporation

The third and last phase of the plot of a wilderness passage rite, the story ending with a beginning, is called *incorporation* (in French, *agrégation*): from the Latin *incorporare*, "to put into the body of something, combine or form into one body, adopt into a body" *(Oxford Dictionary of English Etymology)*. The hero returns from the threshold and is joined with the body of the civilized world, the body of his community. He is incorporated into his new life status. Literally, he takes on his own body. His wandering spirit is seen again in bodily form. He gives birth to himself. He emerges into the social order to become one with the people.

In a psychological sense, the hero is integrating or aggregating. What was threshed is being gathered into a whole, a unity, an identity. The resolution of personal issues extends to the resolution of crisis in the body social. The imbalance in the human environment is being righted. The hero has been "initiated" ("to initiate" is to begin, enter upon, go in, belong). In traditional cultures, the initiate joined all those who had previously passed through the rite. Like them, he now *knew* and was enlightened. Their acceptance of his presence and life story among them validated his quest. This acceptance was automatic. He had fulfilled the initiatory terms. He had successfully passed from one life stage to the next. Now he was qualified to aid in the passage-birth of others, to serve as an "elder" within his new life status, "to perform his vision on earth for the people to see."

Though the return of the modern hero from the threshold is not accompanied by automatic social validation and acceptance, positive therapeutic states are invariably the result. What was once buried now lies open to view. Seeds sown in the "fallow chaos" of the threshold have rooted in the new life.[5] Previously dormant emotions and feelings play upon the surface of consciousness like patterns of light and shadow. Walls and ceilings have tumbled down. Constrictedness has given way to expansiveness, honesty, authenticity. In the flush of ego-strength, the initiate feels ready to take on the world with demonstrations of affection, clear-sightedness, and feelings of personal power or mission.

The absence of social validation can be a crushing blow to one who has just fulfilled the terms of the initiation and who, by all intents and purposes, ought to *belong*. In modern society there is no subculture waiting at the dock to welcome him home. The hero of the modern passage rite must meet with a wall of indifference, as Jumping Mouse did. He must nurse a new life from the stump of the old, from the memory of the Sacred Mountains deep in his heart. Hopefully there will be others who will support his efforts. Even if there is no one to believe him or listen to his story, he will, like Jumping Mouse, set forth on an inner journey, giving away his most precious possessions so that his people will live.

Circles and Mirrors

A long time ago we went to a charitable foundation to ask for scholarships so that graduating high school seniors could celebrate their graduation into adulthood with a wilderness rite of passage. The foundation representative was dubious. "What benefits can there be to going without food and living alone and unprotected in the desert?" she mused. We watched her politely. Things weren't looking too good. She didn't appear to be the type who had ever slept on the ground in a sleeping bag. "What did you call it?" she asked. "A vision quest?" She turned to the anthropologist, a member of our staff. "Describe the benefits of the vision quest," she said. The anthropologist cast us a despairing look, as if to say, "It's futile anyway." She took a piece of paper and drew a circle. "That's the vision quest," she said. Then she drew a dot in the middle of the circle. "That's the vision quester," she added.

We didn't, of course, get the grant. They weren't about to give big bucks to an outfit that starved kids and made them live alone in the inhospitable wilderness. But our anthropologist had a point. The vision quest, fasting quest, and all the other kinds of wilderness passage rites are but circles drawn in the dust, empty forms to be filled with the unique values and perceptions of the participants, mirrors in which they are themselves reflected. Despite all its therapeutic ramifications and potentialities, the transformational power of the passage rite is relative to the person experiencing it. Any assessment of its benefits must begin with an empty circle that is then occupied by a mote of consciousness, a dot of potential, a tiny pinprick of self surrounded by the infinite circle of Self. In other words, the person will not get something for nothing. If there is resolution, it is because the empty circle has been filled with resolution. If there is healing, it is because the circle has been filled with efforts of self-healing. If there is transformation, it is because the circle has been filled with genuine motivation to leave the past behind.

The decision to participate in a fasting quest should not be made lightly, or in the heat of romantic passion. The student should examine his motives, ask himself, "Why do I want to do this?" He should look carefully at his expectations. If, like Prometheus, he wants to steal fire from the sacred altar of vision, what he steals will die in his heart. Does he hope to take a recreational dance through a phantasmagoria of altered states? If so, he will be unable to find a comfortable place to sit. Does he expect a "quickie" transformation, hoping he won't have to work at it too hard? If so, he will return from the Sacred River feeling cheated, puzzled, and no more prepared to serve his people than he was before, having seen in the mirror of nature his own motives reflected. The mirror never lies.

The mystery and beauty of passage rites such as the fasting quest is that they call out the best in the quester. The emptiness, solitude, and exposure challenge the hero in him, tease him into jumping as high as he is able. Since no one else can jump for him, his efforts are genuinely his own. Of course, he is not always aware enough to look before he leaps. He may wind up on a mountain top, or he may wind up in a deep hole. Every story is different, but through every story run the priceless threads of self-understanding.

In every story, however, there is one constant—Grandmother Nature. She bestows her favors, her teachings, her moods, on everyone, regardless of how they perceive her. Some are blinder than others. Some hear better than others. Some learn more quickly than others—but to all she imparts the same information. She covers them all with the same dirt and showers them all with the same rain. Her wisdom voice can be heard in hawk, chuckwalla, kit fox, rattlesnake, scarab beetle, magpie, coyote, tarantula, bighorn sheep, and painted lady butterfly. Her miracles bloom in the cactus, the creosote, the buckwheat, the spruce bush, the desert holly, the evening primrose, the bunch grass, the willow. What the quester choses to see or hear is his business. If he cares to, he can drink the dew of heaven, for Mother Earth sends that, too. Then again, he can try to drink tea, as the following candidate wrote in her threshold journal:

> I had a hard time with the fire and was somewhat discouraged at the fact that all I wanted was one cup of hot tea. I couldn't find the spoon. While looking for it the fire went out. The water was kind of warm. I was going to settle for warm tea when the pot fell into the smoldering fire. I tried again, resorting to toilet paper [as tinder]. The T. P. smoldered. . . .
>
> I am sitting up on this rock, drinking slightly warm instant

tea, which is full of dirt, and there is a bug floating around in it. My hands will have to do in fishing it out. My spoon is still gone. Woe is me.

Needless to say, every initiate returns from the Sacred River with a greater tolerance for dirt and sweat and deeper appreciation for the animal functions of the body. No matter how bad the weather has been, he will wax poetic about the beauty of his place. He will speak of having an odd feeling at certain moments that Mother Earth was aware of him. He might have spent the entire threshold time swatting mosquitoes, nursing blisters, or shivering in his sleeping bag, but his words are filled with gratitude and wonder at her "personalized" care for him. He may even shed tears when he has to leave. A young man, aged twenty-two, recorded such feelings during his threshold fast:

> As I sat on the rocks looking west toward the Sierra, my cry came to me. It went like this: "Mother Earth, please be patient with infant man. We are young and have much to learn. Teach me." That is not exactly what I said, word for word, but is close enough. All the while I got all choked up and began sobbing. Afterwards, I felt a mixture of feelings. The picture of this very old woman, who is very wise, patient, forgiving, sad, and lonely came to me. I think that is what made me cry.

A young Anglo-European woman, aged seventeen, put it another way:

> I feel as if I really do belong out here. How can people who have never experienced nature see her as "Mother?" I must have Indian spirit in me. I have a deep, passionate feeling for the Indians. The land was their mother—as I feel it is for me. Sometimes I wish to God I was an Indian.

"There is only one mother for all people everywhere!" chant the Northern Australian Aborigines in Rainbow Serpent ceremonies celebrating the magnanimous fertility of the earth.[6] This same gift of love for the Great Mother was given to each of us at birth. But we may need to go to her, to fast and be alone with her, before we fully recognize her gift:

In our bones is the rock itself; in our blood is the river;
our skin contains the shadow of every living thing
    we ever came across.
This is what we brought with us long ago. . . .
                —Nancy Wood, "Ute Song"

We prefer to think that modern individuals who participate in wilderness passage rites are not essentially different from their ancestors. Though the cultural circumstances surrounding the passage quest have vastly changed, the experiential, human element has remained constant. We are still capable of hearing the roaring of the Sacred River. We are still capable of talking to Frog. One would be mistaken to assume that we live in a world too far removed from Nature to benefit fully from jumping as high as we are able. From the beginning, the union of human and Nature in passage quest ceremonies has brought forth a healing mythos for the collective woes of the people. We would be foolish to deny ourselves its legacy of self-healing power. We would be helpless indeed if we lost the ability to hear the roaring or the Frog voice— or if, in childish vexation with our brothers and sisters, we destroyed her—for we have no other Mother to "give us, each day, our daily bread."

2

Severance:
Helping
People
Get Ready
to Die

Waiting. If you are sincere,
You have light and success.
Perseverance brings good fortune.
It furthers one to cross the great water.
—*I Ching, "Waiting" (Wilhelm translation)*

Helping a person or group of people prepare for a wilderness rite of passage is a little like helping them get ready to die. The rite will test their readiness to let go of their former life state. In the old days, the preparation phase of a passage rite such as a fasting quest was accorded much attention. The people of the neighborhood all knew that so-and-so was getting ready to undertake the sacred quest, perilous passage, or initiation rite. Perhaps so-and-so had taken a vow or pledge, or had come of age, or had declared his intention to teachers and friends. In some cultures, the candidate went into semiseclusion, entered an apprenticeship, began to observe certain taboos, went to schools taught by elders, or otherwise undertook regimens of preparation. If the quester was to die to his past, he would also have to be ready to be born into his future.

Referring to the ancient Greek mysteries, of which he was an initiate, Aristotle maintained that it was "not necessary for the initiate to learn anything, but to receive impressions and to be put in a certain frame of mind by becoming 'worthy' candidates."[1] The more deathlike the preparation, the more "worthy" the candidate. The "impressions" and "frame of mind" to which Aristotle referred can be seen in many of those who participate in modern passage rites. When the time comes to step across the threshold, they are ready to die. Though their death is the symbolic death of the passage rite, their regimen of preparation has molded them into "worthy" candidates.

The midwife plays an important role in the preparations. Without help, the brave soul entrusted to the midwife's care might not survive the ordeal of symbolic death and rebirth. He might not become a "worthy" candidate.

Decision Road

Every person who elects to participate has consciously placed his feet on decision road, the way that leads ultimately to the purpose circle of death. For this deliberate decision he must be honored, respected, and treated with the same circumspect attention a midwife gives an expectant mother. Not everyone deliberately chooses to sacrifice himself in a symbolic death. The word *sacrifice* is not used flippantly. Symbolic death must involve a sacrifice—an ending. That giving up of oneself to an ending, severance, or parting is, indeed, an enactment of one's real and eventual death.

Most people would simply prefer not to think about decision road, or their inevitable death. Better to hide the absolute certainty of it with illusions of present safety, comfort, and convenience. Better to put the feet anywhere but on decision road. Hence, they are captured unaware by all the symbolic deaths the living of their life brings. At every transition they must sacrifice something of themselves. Giving up a part of themselves while at all costs avoiding decision road invariably turns them into victims, problems, liabilities, imbalances in the social order. Many stuck in their passages never get out.

The deliberateness of the pace of the severance phase is calculated to draw out and refine the quality of preparedness, to produce Aristotle's "certain frame of mind." The midwife's task is to provide an adequate regimen by which initiates may formalize their decision to give themselves to an ending.

Preparing for the Death Passage

A wilderness fast of three to six days and nights in perfect solitude requires at least a half-year of preparation, particularly if it is geared to individuals in life crisis. Although preparation on the physical plane is of most importance (the death is only symbolic), the behavior of the initiate in the physical world is affected by other states as well: his psychological makeup, his mental and perceptual attitude, and his spiritual beliefs and values. Every part of his life is affected by the decision to undertake a vision fast. If these parts are not aligned and attuned to the completion of the passage, then difficulties will arise, even disaster. When the time has come, a midwife must feel confident that the quester has prepared well before allowing him to be alone at the Sacred River.

It is absolutely necessary to meet with those who are scheduled to participate, to speak with them of personal matters, imparting necessary information, assessing their readiness to die symbolically. The content of meetings and kinds and methods of instruction may vary widely, according to the type of threshold ordeal, the life crisis or transition being marked, the threshold area, the time of year, and so on. Certain themes run through every quester's preparations. Even as they prepare to die symbolically, they prepare to live, to survive. In a wilderness rite, personal and group survival, hazards of time and place, adequate equipment, environmental awareness, emergency procedures, and other matters pertinent to the ordeal must be taken up.[2]

"Psychological" facets of preparation include readiness to sever from the former life and to take on the new. Every participant must be given an opportunity to express fears, anxieties, expectations, feelings, and clarified intentions to resolve unfinished issues in the past, to imagine the new life status into which he will be incorporated. As he draws near the threshold, his readiness can often be measured by his willingness to introspect, to negotiate the inward landscape of feelings. There is therapeutic ore in the dark mountains of introspection, a self-honesty more precious than gold. Decision road invariably leads to what is deepest and most dear within oneself and one's world.

Intellectual preparation involves teaching concepts, symbols, allegories, assigning reading material, using self-monitoring techniques (journal, diary), and understanding in overview the personal steps to be taken throughout the passage ceremony, from commitment to return, ending to beginning. Myths or folk tales can be introduced to good advantage. Simple concepts and symbols, often linked to wilderness passage rites, are discussed later in the text.

Mytho-spiritual preparation and introduction to the sacred mysteries has always attended passage rites. Jung has closely examined the intimate connection between "spiritual" and "psychological."[3] Much of the preparation involving matters of individual faith or conviction may have decidedly Jungian overtones. It is vitally necessary that the modern initiate be psychologically prepared within his own value system, that he find or possess symbolic tools, personal myths about himself and his relationship to a personal deity or force, that will abet his threshold passage and establish his place on the other side. If he appears to be lacking the mytho-spiritual dimensions, then he must become sensitized to the interpretation of events of his life from an allegorical and symbolic perspective.

The Death Lodge

When little Mouse first decided to investigate the roaring in his ears, he entered decision road, the road that leads to death. Leaving Mouseland behind, he never quite made it back. Likewise the initiate. Once he has dared to trust in decision road, he must eventually come to where it leads, to a little house apart from the village where people go when they want to tell everyone they are ready to die.

Death lodge preparation involves going to that little house (it can be an actual place on the earth) and entertaining all those from one's past who come to say goodbye. This of course does not mean that actual people come. The old medicine man would say, "Their spirits come."

One by one the dying person entertains these spirits or "karmic ghosts" of his past, giving and asking forgiveness. If forgiveness is not forthcoming, the dying person must accept their refusal and go on. If he cannot forgive, then he must accept his own reluctance and go on.

He must not spend too much time at one stretch in the death lodge. When carried on too long, the ceremony can be an exhausting, debilitating process. Spaced over a week's time, the death lodge is an effective means of alleviating the karmic load. Values, convictions, personal myths stand out in bold relief against the background of past events. That which does not fall away will enrich the spiritual placenta on which his birthing spirit will feed when he is in the uterus of the threshold passage.

Decision road does not stop, however, at the little house at the edge of the village. It leads to the purpose circle on the mountain, to the dying place, where the initiate goes beyond the realm of the living to the hope of birth. There he will stand alone. No one will go with him into the fallow darkness, where death will teach him about giving himself.

The Therapeutics of Risk

Fear tests commitment, will, and patience. Fear of death (real or imagined), as in a passage rite, tempts the candidate to turn back. The former life crisis, which he is committed to end, looks more and more desirable. He questions his desire to participate, wondering whatever got him to do such a crazy thing. He doesn't feel ready to come out of his hole. He remembers all the times he was weak or a "failure." Demons set free by his own imagining lurk in the shadows. If he becomes too frightened, he will abort his own "coming forth by daylight."

The fear is *real.* It's not a scary movie. The one who is preparing can't make the anxiety go away by shutting his eyes or covering his ears. The midwife must make sure he can safely deal with his fears during the wilderness passage. Fear manifests itself in forms of behavior that don't necessarily indicate unsuitability for the rite. Trembling hands can still do what is necessary. Shaking knees can still carry one to safety. The most fearful student may be the steadiest in a crisis, the best at engaging the direct fury of the monster.

> This shaking keeps me steady, I should know.
> I learn by going where I have to go.
> —Theodore Roethke, "The Waking"

As the threshold looms, the candidate tends to become candid about his life situation. Pretenses will be dropped; habitual falsehoods will no longer seem necessary. Emotions just beneath the surface will surge at the first scratch. Unmasked by fear, he will become genuine, unique, an infinitely beautiful and fragile mortal. This vulnerability is fertile soil. Good counsel and empathetic sharing can be planted in it. Under no circumstance should this emotional nakedness be made shameful. He must be helped to link up with that tight knot in his belly, as he might link up with an ally. The best way to do that is not to shield him from his fears, or to compound them, but to share weaknesses, humanness, with him. The ordeal of passage is not a macho game played to see who can be the bravest or most stoic. An old adage goes, "The greater the fear, the greater the blessing."

Sometimes the little Mouse will hide his fear. He will assume a conditioned persona or mask that suppresses rather than integrates the fear. Recognizable fear personas include: the happy-go-lucky boy who will try anything if there is risk in it; the strong, silent man, rugged enough to take the hardest knocks; the crazy little girl out for kicks who will do anything on a dare; the maternal, responsible type who looks after everyone else's business but her own. Anger can also be an effective fear mask, irrationally striking out at others to hide the apprehension inside. Conversely, smiling, serene unattachment to emotion can hide the deepest, most debilitating apparitions of fear.

Those who cannot dance gracefully with their fears will often screen themselves out of the severance process. They realize they are not ready to undertake the ordeal. But those who hide their fears from themselves are often stripped of their masks of avoidance after they have crossed the threshold boundary. This can be dangerous. Consider the fate of the fifty-year-old man who overtaxed himself with a long hike, trying to prove that he was as young as ever. All alone, miles from help, he confronted the monster of a heart attack. Consider the lot of the young woman who forgot to confess that she had been entertaining thoughts of suicide. She almost turned her symbolic death into a real one when she wandered into a maze of canyons that led her, hopelessly lost for two days and nights, into a living nightmare of somehow holding on, wanting to live, wanting to be found by a rescue party. Consider the dilemma of the young man who hid his fear of loneliness so well that, in order to avoid the loneliness of his ordeal, he manufactured a crisis that would bring him back to basecamp. He jumped off a nearly vertical slope, starting a landslide that should have killed him. Miraculously unhurt, he walked into basecamp, feigning a limp.

For the keen-eyed teacher, there are many "windows" through which the initiate can be seen in some characteristic pose or gesture that reveals his way of perceiving the world. Through the window of fear, he is seen either pared down to the bare bones of his life story, or holding up an illusory face, a means or gesture of avoidance, a mythical face that will shred in the first cold wind. One can only listen and watch, intent on the personal drama of severance, edified by what each candidate teaches. Every bit of information is important. The final decision, to allow or not to allow the initiate to cross the threshold, is up to the midwife. He must not allow himself to be influenced by thoughts of "It will do him good to go through this." The objective of symbolic death is survival.

Preparing to Fast

People of ancient times went without food more often than average modern Americans. It was no real hardship to fast for a few days during a passage rite. To the prohibition of food they often added companionship, shelter, clothing, even water. Extremes were sometimes reached with self-mutilation—piercing, branding, amputation of a finger, circumcision, subincision. Such actions hardly seem necessary in modern America, where people are scared if they miss a single meal. To the vast majority, the idea of voluntarily giving up sustenance (and/or water, shelter, companionship) for several days and nights, sleeping empty and alone with the creepie-crawlies, is the zenith of insanity. Who cares if Jesus, Moses, Mohammed, or the Buddha did it? That was in the old days. Nowadays, if you act too much like Jesus, you wind up in the nuthouse.

Fasting, solitude, and exposure to nature constitute an adequate modern ordeal. Although such a trial is a piece of cake for a few, for the many it smacks of a kind of death. Fasting, particularly, is a monster, though mainly a psychological one. Greater risks lie in physical isolation and exposure to unbridled elements. Nevertheless, the greatest fears of the threshold usually involve going without food. The fear of being empty points out the profound role of plenitude in "the great American dream."

Initiates can prepare for a fast by practicing "going without," not easily done when surrounded by the tempting goodies of civilization. You might suggest they remove themselves from all normal contacts during their practice periods. The medicine walk, for example (see below), is "fasting practice" incorporated into a twelve-hour ceremony. If they face a food-*and*-water fast, then it behooves them to practice going without water as well.

Traditional preparation for fasting includes abstention from alcohol, drugs, or other substances that accumulate toxins in the body. There are also taboos against the ingestion of rich or gluttonous foods. The severance phase is a time to purify the body—and,

37

by extension, the spirit. Initiates might also stay away from heavy meats, oily or fried foods, dairy or poultry products, nuts, or anything that is hard to digest and tends to build up sludge in organs, tissues, and blood. Concomitant with dietary preparation is good physical condition, tuning the body to the threshold ordeal with running, walking, cycling, or aerobics. Ordinarily, questers know when they are out of shape. If they can't cover a level mile without getting out of breath, they are not physically ready.

The Medicine Walk

The medicine walk, a day's journey upon the face of the earth, is a microcosmic life story. As a ceremony of preparation, the walk is a mirror. Signs and symbols of the walker's inward journey are reflected by the natural environment. If he takes his medicine walk one month before the threshold, he will have adequate time to digest the experience and to use it as an allegorical guide to his preparations.

The person walks a full day, from the rising to the setting of the sun, in a natural place devoid, if possible, of people. During his walk he goes without food (but not without water, unless prearranged). Though he must inform someone of his whereabouts (in case he doesn't return), he otherwise walks alone. He should wear appropriate clothing and carry a daypack for emergency items. If he is a tenderfoot, he must make his walk a conservative one, staying close to his vehicle or familiar landmarks. The object is not to get lost. No matter how far he roams he should be back by sunset. (The medicine walk may be difficult for women living in urban areas where there can be heavy male predation. It is usually possible to find a solution to this problem.)

The walk should be canceled if the weather prohibits it. The idea is not to endanger life and limb or to challenge the elements, but to meander like a river along a self-directed course. The walker does not have to keep walking all day. He can stop, look, or rest whenever he wishes. As he wanders, he will sense nature's awareness of him. Signs and symbols indicating his life purpose, inherent gifts, personal values, or private fears, will present themselves. He will see the beauty of life and the reality of death in the world of his true mother. He must ask himself, "Who are my people?" and pay attention to those who come to him during this time (who he thinks about, worries about, obtains strength or courage from). The "spirits" of these people may become part of his purpose circle of symbolic death.

The midwife helps the student read the "story" of his medicine walk and shows him how it might reflect on his life quest. The more the walker ponders the meaning of the symbols he encounters, the deeper and richer the remaining days of his severance preparation will be.

The Journal

Initiates must be encouraged to use journals or other means of self-documentation, making entries every day. If they are utterly honest with themselves, they will reap the benefits in self-insight, and will become accustomed to traveling the inner space of symbolic death. The monsters will be there, as well as the heroes to do battle with them. Their reasons for questing will appear, as well as their deepest prayers and dreams.

Keeping a journal is one thing. Valuing insights gained therefrom is something else. A young woman once returned from her medicine walk with a journal filled with beautiful self-analysis, claiming that "nothing happened," that "none of my questions were answered." We pointed out to her that many of the answers to her life questions were right there in her journal account. "Oh that," she shrugged. "That's just me." Apparently, "just me" wasn't enough. Such insights were worthless because they were written by "just me." The ready interest of an "elder" in the internal affairs of a journal will help the writer to gather courage and faith in himself as a "worthy candidate."

Jumping Under Your Own Power

With his own legs, little Mouse jumped as high as he could and saw the Sacred Mountains shining in the distance. So the initiate must jump, with his own values, beliefs, and perceptions guiding him. It is important that he study and practice jumping styles ahead of time, so that he knows which way is best for him. He doesn't want to wind up flat-footed at the edge of the great river.

The midwife's task is to help him find ceremonial ways to mark, formalize, or celebrate whatever life change he has in mind, and to use symbolic tools compatible with his belief system. Since no priest, minister, medicine man, or guru will be there to tell him what to do or how to do it, any gesture or thing he choses to call sacred will be sacred. He may be curious about how he will go about expressing himself in a sacred mode.

He may need to ponder and talk about the power and nature of ceremony, about its three phases (severance, threshold, incorporation); how it links two orders of reality, the sacred and profane; how it invests with significance and generates and reinforces commitment; how it is an ancient means of communicating with the spirits of those invoked. Some might innocently believe that performance of ceremony takes care of a problem or resolves a crisis forever. They miss the point. Ceremony is something done in real time and space that persists in the memory only as long as the celebrant holds it there. On the other hand, a million years of time will not retract a ceremony. It may not resolve the crisis, but the focused intent to do so has been indelibly stitched on the fabric of the universe.

The candidate has much ritual material at his disposal: singing, chanting, drumming, rattling, and all the other ways to make music. There is perfect silence to focus intent and observe being, to listen to the "still, small voice." There is motion: dancing, walking, climbing, descending, kneeling, skipping, jumping, gesturing, and sitting still. There are means of empowering symbols: blood, fire, spit, urine, sweat, water, mud, cornmeal, tobacco, incense, ochre, herbs, ashes, sunlight, moonlight, and dawn. There are offerings of honey, water, wine, grain, hair, flesh, blood, tobacco, song, dance, silence, and prayer. There are all the ritual actions: burying, burning, smashing, name changing, cutting of hair, aligning or heaping of stones, smudging, and going naked. There are the ways of "calling in" ancestors, teachers, parents, loved ones, friends, ghosts, spirits, naiads, and other unseen presences to witness the ceremony. There are the mask makings, the body paintings, the costume changings, the psychodramas, the ablutions, baptisms, and rebirthings. All these and more are available to him.

Of course, he must realize that he will be all alone, exposed and empty, performing his ceremony in a natural place. Nature has her own teaching agenda. In truly miserable or dangerous weather, he must think twice about proceeding with a ceremony. It may be that Mother Nature is not filling the heavens with her fury just so he can prove he is a courageous fool. The storm itself may be conducting the ceremony.

A few years ago, a fasting woman was threatened by a granddaddy of a lightning storm just as she'd begun a special dance atop an exposed ridge in Death Valley. She had not danced more than a few steps when she realized it was Lightning who preferred to dance. She retreated in the nick of time. This decision probably saved her life.

On the other hand, one does not scuttle carefully laid plans just because the wind is cold or clouds are gathering. The quester must ask: "What kind of self-discipline does this ceremony require of me?"

Some tend to be more ceremony-minded than others. They must be cautioned against filling every waking hour with ritual behavior. Too many rich meals are hard to digest. Nor is a ceremony the antidote to boredom any more than makeup is the antidote to nakedness. Ceremonial attention can mask the essential experience of the moment. The ceremonialist forgets about the existence of the profane, or physical, and the ceremony loses its balance.

The following accounts from the threshold journals of questers illustrate both formal and informal aspects of self-generated ceremony. Each account represents an attempt to resolve a personal crisis or transition within the greater whole of the threshold passage.

> I see the importance of milestone events. This ceremony involves masks of papier mâché, exact likenesses of my face. The two masks are quite different, however. One represents my life up to now. The eyes are closed, as are the nose and mouth. This posture of my face represents my past life, which I remember as gray and restricted by my own choice. I feared many things, was blind to most sensations—a defense against family life, which accompanied me everywhere, letting nothing or no one come close.
>
> I'm not quite sure how I've come to be the man I am today, but I feel I've grown out of much of my childhood. The second mask, the one that represents the man and the future I am

heading towards, is a proud, beautiful mask. It fits like a glove over my real face. The eyes are open, as are the ears and mouth. The edge is radiant, like the sun, reaching out in all directions. When I wear this mask, the eye-holes are cut in such a way that I must hold my head high in proud fashion in order to see. . . . It is an open mask, willing to face the unknown. It feels and listens and sees children as the place to plant the truth.

Thinking of my early life brings me to say these words to my childhood mask: "I am strong enough now to stand alone. I have outgrown you. You no longer fit, so I must leave you here on this cold mountain top. Do not despair. I have made a new mask which you have had a hand in making. See there? The face is the same . . . but this mask is also different from you. Its eyes are open. It is colorful and eager to feel both good and painful. . . . You need not feel sad, for you lay a foundation for this new layer of manhood. There will be new layers to follow."

Today, I leap beyond my childhood. As a man, I vow to become compassionate, strong, truthful, giving—in other words, myself. I have a good direction and many good teachers to learn from. I know I shall not falter. With all my life, good-bye. With all my eagerness and hope, hello! My chosen name is Earth Son.

—Earth Son, twenty-two

Last night I went on a rampage, turning into a cave woman, destroying pieces of dead timber. I just took large pieces of dead wood and clubbed them against the rocks. . . . Actually I could never describe the satisfaction that I got from beating those pieces of wood against the rocks. It was great. I never felt anything like it. If the wood didn't break, then I just put all my might into it until it did. I screamed a little too, but not too much. I hurt my hands a lot but that didn't matter. In fact, in a funny way, it even felt good. I must have done that for thirty to forty minutes, nonstop. I am thankful to have found a spot where something like that could be accomplished in the night with nobody else to see me just going around picking up dead logs and bashing them against the rocks. . . .

It happened all of a sudden and left as quickly as it came. But I will remember it for a long while. Hopefully, I will never let myself get so pent up with frustration again, but if I do I pray for another chance to let it out.

—Night Stalker, thirty-two

I was afraid when I thought of death, so I decided to make a death stick to talk to and perhaps burn. It was a solid piece of wood and its eyes were dark and slit-like. I said to it: "Death, I want to speak to you. I have searched for you at times."

"You are not ready," said Death.

"I have wanted to die."

"Die then, and let go of the idea."

"Death, I respect you. I will burn the suicidal thoughts. Death, I will put you in the fire."

I put Death in the fire and the fire died. I got a little panicky then, thinking I had to relight it quickly. I lit four matches before it started again.

I spoke to the wind. "Wind, be gentle, or this stick will not burn."

I thought about Death. Death killed the flame again. I was unable to relight the fire. I cried. I was afraid. I wanted it to burn. I moved the coals with my fingers.

"You can't get rid of me. I will always be here waiting. But *you* must be ready," said Death.

I stopped stirring the coals and let the fire die. I had no more matches. I asked the coals to give me a name. They caught fire with a blue light. I listened, but there was nothing. The flame died. I asked again and again. I left my mind open. Nothing. I gave up and asked the spirit if I could stay there the night. I asked for a power dream. I set up my sleeping bag and watched the coals, thinking of my friends and family. The coals began to hum and crackle. I listened. Blue flames caught again, and the renewed fire sang its song. "Quiet Blue Fire Sings?" I asked the fire. It died, again. The wind sang: "No, wait."

—Comes From Two Places, seventeen

How to reflect on yesterday. I did a medicine dance. I literally flew over those mountains, shouting, screeching like an eagle. Many prayers to the four directions. This is the most magnificent place I have ever seen. . . . Surely, this is a sacred place. It was hot—I only had a small canteen of water. But I went so far—four ridges up, four ridges over, to the mother mountain of the canyons themselves, the headlands of the Owl's Head [Mountains]. Precipices, rocks, plants, animal holes. The place was alive with hidden life, vibrant with spirits of all dimensions. Every rock and shrub had a story, a message. In the desolation of my spirit, the natural world had a very clear voice. . . . It said, "The earth is your inheritance."

—Laughing Eagle, thirty-four

I built a fire and started my ceremony of release from mourning for my deceased love affair. I have brought out the last remains—a packet of hair—and I write a letter of commitment to the joy that was and my need to transform the bound feelings, to release them and be renewed. The actions sink deeply into the sacred tissues of my grief. I cry. I beseech the guiding spirit to help me learn and let go. The hair and paper sizzle in the tiny fire, consumed, dissolved. I am peaceful again. A red moon rises.

—Barking Dog, twenty-six

Here I sit in my "coffin"—wearing the ring. . . . It reminds me that I implored God to teach me to love twenty-four years ago, and His answer was the Bond. So the myth of the Bond is grounded in devotion to the Most High, heretical as it may seem to some, and fragile and self-deceiving as it seems to me in times of doubt. And I find a kind of comfort and a real release in knowing I have vowed myself to celibacy. No more wonderings—no more feelings that I "ought" to be open. I am not open to anything but the Bond, wherever that may take me in finishing up its business, consuming and channeling its remaining energy. . . .

Asked the moon's blessing on the ring—holding it up in the moonlight and turning it slowly so all of it was shone on. Asked the power of serenity and peace in the One. The moon is so *one!* The sun is active, warm, light, and *many*—its rays are like the myriad forms of creation. . . .

But the moon is single, one, complete. Peace. Death. One. . . .

It came to me that the Bond would no longer exist at my death. A bond exists between two separate beings, binding them together into a whole. At my death, [my husband] and I will be drawn into a single unit that our closeness on earth was but a foretaste of.

—Gift Bearer, fifty-nine (confirming the bond between herself and her dead husband)

44

Goodbye to Mouseland

Decision road leads away from Mouseland, away from familiar precincts and a former life context. Traditionally, the initiates are removed from a society and taken as a group to the place where the rite will take place. This penultimate step in severance is accompanied by a drawing together of the group under a common purpose. In anticipation of the giving away of self required by the threshold's symbolic death, questers might be expected to share duties and responsibilities and fully participate in the group's activities.

The presence of elders (those who have already experienced the rite and are acting as guides) among the initiates is absolutely necessary. In native cultures, these elders were duly authorized to instruct the initiates, not only in the intricacies of the rite, but in the requirements and responsibilities of the life change they were celebrating. Modern elders serve a similar function. Of course, they do not lord it over the candidates. They give themselves to them with questions, information, instruction, and love, so that the birth will be successful.

Once the initiate leaves the village, they are Raccoon's responsibility. He sees how vulnerable they are, how fear writes stories in their faces. Now more than ever he sees the wisdom of the ancient ritualistic ways of bringing forth into a new life station. How little he really has to do. They are being pulled along by the gravitational forces of the ceremony itself, in the inexorable grip of the third trimester. They are gravid with incipient change. Remembering his own fear and excitement, the midwife honors theirs.

He may choose to bring the group to singleness of intent with ceremonies of singing, dancing, or shared discussion, remembering that a group can be distracted all too easily if the ceremony makes them feel uncomfortable or they are uncertain about the parts they play. The aim is not only to bring coherence to heterogeny but to instill a sense of personal meaning through participation.

Initial contact with the threshold area, especially by tenderfeet, can be negative. Intellectually, they can assent to the idea that nature is their true mother. Emotionally, they feel dislocated, uncomfortable, and apprehensive. Tempers may flare, irrational fears mount. Where are the palm trees, the babbling brooks, the verdant oases, the Alpine scenery? "It doesn't look like what I imagined." "Symbolic death out here? What an unappealing notion!" "What kind of creature lives in that hole? What if it slithers out at night and visits me?" "You didn't tell me there would be so many insects." "I'm dirty already. Where's the shower?" "God, how I miss my home and friends!"

Their fears can be honored by asking them separately or as a group to express in some positive way their bond to the earth. Through ceremonies of gratitude, honor, or respect for the earth, anxieties may be stilled and the lingering spirits of those who lived here before propitiated. At the outset, gratitude expressed to the spirits for safekeeping will instill a positive outlook. Reminded by commitment and intent, the group will draw together again into common purpose.

Severing the Last Cord

The threshing-hold is at hand. The time to die has come. The initiate is about to enter the fabled zone of power, the sacred world of fasting, solitude, and exposure, bounded at the four horizons by the natural world. The first act of the drama of his passage into newness has ended. Now the curtain will rise on the second act. He will live "betwixt and between," fixed on a deathward journey into birth.

Traditionally, the initiate crosses the threshold at sunrise. His last hours are marked by actions calculated to sever him completely from his former life station. One last time he is asked to share his deepest fears before he goes where there is no human contact. One last time he touches others with hugs and words of encouragement before he goes where there is no human comfort. One last time he surveys the scene at basecamp, the midwives, the equipment, the food, before he goes where emptiness gnaws at the belly. One last time he holds hands and sings "We are one with the infinite sun/ forever and ever and ever" before he goes into the all-mothering world of wordlessness.

A threshold circle is drawn in the dust. This circle represents the tunnel, the door, through which the initiate will exit the former world. Once he has entered this circle, he cannot be touched by any person who stays outside the border. He assumes his spirit body and rapidly becomes "invisible" to the corporeal eye. One last time he looks his midwife in the face. The waiting is over. Now it is time "to cross the great water." No word will suffice but "Goodbye." Encircled by his life purpose, he steps into the tunnel and is gone. The crunch of his bootsteps fades into the sound of roaring, the roaring of the Sacred River.

3

"Do You Want Some Medicine?"

You say nothing is created new?
Don't worry about it, with the mud
of the earth, make a cup
from which your brother can drink.
—*Antonio Machado, "Moral Proverbs and Folk*
Songs"

"Would you like to have some Medicine power?" was the question posed by Mother Nature's spirit, the Frog. He was addressing the little Mouse trembling at the brink of the great river. "Yes, yes!" came the eager reply. Now, Frog had been assessing Mouse's "medicine gifts." With his shrewd, bulging eyes he could see what Mouse was good at doing. When he told him, "Jump as high as you are Able!" he was not, however, simply referring to Mouse's powerful back legs. He was also referring to Mouse's ability to attain what was best in himself. And when Mouse jumped and saw the Sacred Mountains, he was seeing into the distance of his own heart.

"Medicine," as we will define it, is only incidentally a prescription to cure a problem. Mouse was in a crisis. But he didn't jump to see the cause of his crisis. He jumped and saw the eventual outcome of all this crisis business—the visionary mountains. He saw that his momentary "problem" was but a landmark along the long crooked road of his life. He would face far worse crises than the roaring in his ears. Again and again he would be called upon to use the "medicine" the Frog gave him, jumping as high as he was able.

A classic definition of medicine and its relationship to self-healing was made by the American Indian holy man, Black Elk:

> We should understand well that all things are the works of the Great Spirit. We should know that He is within all things: the trees, the grasses, the rivers, the mountains, and all the four-legged animals, and the winged peoples; and even more important, we should understand that He is also above all these things and peoples. When we do understand all this deeply in our

51

hearts, then we will fear, and love, and know the Great Spirit, and then we will be and act and live as He intends.[1]

The "within-ness" of the Great Spirit in all the manifestations of Mother Nature, including the human, is the source of good medicine. This withinness connects human to nature. At the interface between spirit-indwelt nature and spirit-indwelt human, the medicine teacher dances. In the story, Raccoon was a "medicine teacher." He introduced little Mouse to Frog. Frog and Mouse talked. Mouse got his medicine power. And that's how it works. . . . But in practice it's not quite that simple.

If you want to be a medicine teacher, then you must start with our master teacher, Mother Nature. You must go to her and learn from her and never stop learning from her. You must console yourself with the realization that never will you know enough. After fifty years or so, you may, however, reach Raccoon's level of proficiency. As for us, we know nothing. That's why we presume to write boldly about this subject in the first place. What we do know is that medicine teaching is as effective, if not more, than conventional psychotherapeutic methods. We have seen the results, and have ceased to marvel, accepting them, rather, as the norm.

The real secret is that the midwife or teacher does very little. All he has to do is introduce Mouse to the Sacred River and to Frog. Mother Nature does the rest. She does all the work. She takes care of little Mouse's "problem." She shows him the Sacred Mountains.

"If you have not lived through something, it is not true," says Robert Bly in *The Kabir Book*. The way you practice "medicine" begins with your *own* experience of the concrete, real, sentient, and nonsentient forms of the earth. You cannot earn your credentials by reading nature books. Add to your experience a careful, attentive mind. Another ingredient must be included: imagination, imagination of the truth, that, as William Blake put it, "Everything that lives is holy." Imagination that a little ball of rabbit dung is as holy as an eagle circling the sky or a tree full of angels singing "Glory, glory." And if you have patiently watched yourself experiencing nature, imagining the truth of the indwellingness of the Spirit in all things, you will have discovered a different level of reality, a reality of coincidence, synchronicity, allegory, sign, symbol, and dream, the stuff of the threshold world of the wilderness rite of passage.

As Raccoon introduced Mouse to the Sacred River and to Frog, so the "medicine midwife" helps another to enter and make sense of the wilderness threshold. By "make sense of" we mean, find that within himself that listens and responds to the voice of indwelling nature, the voice that prompts him to jump as high as he is able. Of course, one cannot even begin to help a person on this level unless one has already listened to that voice, and heeded its prompting to give away what has been found. The midwife needs to be able to say, "I know there is an indwelling presence in all things and I have communed with it. I honor and respect its power and wisdom and seek this presence wherever I go."

The midwife cannot use the ways of nature to help someone else without being intimately acquainted with her ways. Textbooks, graduate courses, and scientific laws hardly constitute an "intimate acquaintance." There are so many other ways to know her, ways involving blindness, emptiness, incomprehension, awe, supernal clarity, love, and madness. There are the ways of barely hanging on by the skin of one's teeth in the thundering gale of death. There are the ways of knowing her with one's guts, with loose bowels and panting sweat, with the survival hunger of the animal. There are the ways of stillness and solitude, of no-thought, no-feeling, no-sense. There are the ways of sensuality, of surrendering to the look and feel and touch of her, of falling under her sacred spell. There are the ways of conversing with her, living and communicating with her creatures, attuned to her voice with the ear of the Great Spirit. If such as these are among your ways of knowing her, then you might consider how your knowing can be used to help heal your people.

Good Medicine and Psychotherapy

A candidate in a wilderness passage rite may confess that his life is joyless, his fatherhood a failure, his family life a private hell, his future bleak. Or she may say that she has left her husband, that she is out on her own, a working mother with nowhere to go. Or he may appear in the deepest distress because he is under the thrall of liquor or a drug and is in despair of ever throwing it off his back. Whatever the crisis, their former lives may be like ashes in their mouths, their hopes scattered to the whirlwind. Their sense of self-worth may not amount to a row of beans. They probably won't be able to assess how much they have already learned or how far along life's path they have already come, for their lives have narrowed down to a dark passageway and all they can see is the gloom.

Cognitive, behavioral, and social psychologies would treat the person's problem, concentrating on the underlying causes of his unhappiness. A treatment plan might be drawn up, a healing regimen, a prescription aimed at alleviating the distress. The problem would be processed by therapeutic strategies. Thoughts, feelings, and emotions would be grouped together or typed according to particular behavioral profiles. The client would become dependent on the therapist for necessary repairs to his psyche. Most likely, the therapy would focus on *what's wrong,* on the negative complex that inhibited the client from realizing his full potential.

In the story of Jumping Mouse, the Frog sitting on the lily pad didn't seem to care what was wrong with the little Mouse, or at least he didn't show much concern. And his prescription automatically disqualified him from being much of a therapist. He simply saw what Mouse was good at doing and told him to do it. There was, of course, a stipulation. Mouse had to do it in the great outside world, beside the Sacred River, where Dame Nature herself would provide the therapy.

Medicine work involves a kind of trickery—hence its association with sorcery or shamanism. The trick is to get out of the way so that nature and human nature can do the work. But this getting out of the way involves some work on the midwife's part. He should forget about trying unless he has earned his getting-out-of-the-way credentials from the Wilderness University. If he has accreditation, then he might have an idea of how he could "set up" an initiate within a framework, grid, or process oriented to the natural world, a form in which Mouse can find empowerment through interaction with nature.

Again, the fable holds an important clue about how medicine works. In his crisis, Mouse turned to the natural world, seeking answers to his questions, resolution to his discontent. And all around him were bits and pieces of the world, carried along in the current of the great river. What Mouse didn't know at the time was that the Sacred River of nature is a mirror which reflects the symbols, shapes, images, signs, and myths of he who looks into the mirror. Specifically, what Mouse saw when he looked into the mirror of the Sacred River was Frog. Now Frog himself was no belly-crawler. He was a jumper, just like Mouse; just the sign Mouse had been looking for, a natural reflection/projection of his own ability to jump. In a sense, Mouse "created" Frog; he made him appear. He would never have seen him if he hadn't decided to go down to the Sacred River.

When a human being is put into a natural context, into his real home, within an allegorical framework that includes his symbolic death, disturbances occur in the ordinary flow of consciousness, subtly altered states of awareness, heightened emotions, intuitive reactions, perceptual crises, psychic perturbations. Cracks appear in the shell of conditioning. There is some ego loss. Then there is a regaining of balance, a drawing together into a tougher, grounded whole, a psychic integration. It is as though the gravitational force of the old life ceases to hold things together as the subject comes under the coherent force of the new life. Betwixt the old and the new, the subject is open to interpretations of his life story, ways of seeing into the mirror, ways of finding self-validation in natural symbols and processes.

Because the medicine teacher lives at the psycho-symbolic interface of human and Nature, he walks a path both profane and spiritual. He knows that the higher agrees with the lower, that the microcosm of self contains the macrocosm of Self, that a single hour spent in Nature contains the germs of a life story, that "Within everything is the seed of everything" (Hermetic axiom). Part of the preparation of the initiate is to offer him ways of interacting with the mirror of his true Mother.

Another part comes when the initiate returns from the psycho-symbolic terrain of the wilderness threshing-hold. At that point the midwife must be there to point out the story, plot, or drama of his threshold experience, to identify the gifts, assets, powers, and allies that aided him in his heroic journey, to ask, as Frog did, "What did you see?" and to verify the medicine power within him: "And you have a new name! It is Jumping Mouse!"

Blinded at the Threshold

Greek mythology has it that Tiresias, the famed Theban sooth-sayer, when a young man, went hiking alone in the deep forest behind his home. He came upon a forbidden sight. Athene, the goddess and the companion of his mother, was bathing in a spring. Angry that mortal eyes should see her naked, she blinded him. But then she took pity on him and gave him compensatory gifts; the power to understand the language of birds, the power to foresee the future, and a cornel-wood staff to serve as his eyes.[2]

Let us begin with the young man, Tiresias, the initiate into adulthood. The deep woods are the threshold. Athene, patroness of wisdom, navigation, the olive tree, and the earthen pot, is the Goddess of the Earth, Mother Earth. Though the young man's encounter with the goddess seems accidental, the truth is he must be blinded if he is to attain the next stage of his life.

In the threshing-hold of Nature, the initiate must lose his rational perception. He must go inside himself, into the blindness of intuition and instinct, where compensatory gifts await him, conferred by the goddess. As he gropes his way through this world of feeling and introspection, he learns to yield to the rhythms and forces of Nature, to watch himself through the inner eyes of self-consciousness, to navigate psychological space, to communicate with the creatures, to hearken to the in-dwelling spirit in all things, to know what lies between emotion and thought, fear and understanding, to hear the voices of his collective ancestors. The goddess teaches him by scaring him. She brushes death up close to him so that he will acquire death power. She holds up her mirrorlike shield, in which only the blind may see.

Seeing with Other Eyes

With the language of logic, we can arrive at the conclusion that other creatures besides us possess nonhuman intelligence. But we cannot speak the language of logic to dolphins or coyotes or coela-canths or boll weevils, nor, with the ear of logic, can we hear what they say to us. How little we know about the intelligence and consciousness of other species!

We are led to believe a lie
When we see not through the Eye.
—William Blake, "Auguries of Innocence"

The medicine teaching of early cultures often presumed that there was intelligence in all the other creatures, and a means of communicating with them via the sacred spirit-bond interconnecting every child of Mother Earth. If someone has earned his credentials by living among the spirits of the wilderness, he knows this teaching is true. He also knows that Gaia has a way of ignoring his rational, conditioned perceptions of her. There are too many coincidences, too many anamolies, too many illogical—and deeply meaningful—confrontations, too many riddles and puzzles to which there are no answers. He knows she has ways of humbling him, robbing him of speech and thought, or making him grovel and scratch like any other animal. He knows how suddenly, unexpectedly, she changes her mind, turns her savage, indifferent face, and visits him with a lightning storm, an earthquake, a tornado, or a flash flood. Above all, he has come to feel her awareness of him; he respects the signs and symbols she places in his path. When he goes to her he goes to listen and to learn.

Those who have entered the threshing-hold often describe experiences of nonordinary reality. A raven speaks to them, an eagle answers a prayer, a tree fruits with insight, a primrose unfolds an illumination, an ant brings wisdom, an apparition appears; they are visited by an ancestor, spun around by a hallucination, touched by a power animal, ally, spirit guide, ghost, or demon. They discover a part of themselves that they did not know existed. They are frightened, intrigued, awed, dazzled, uncomprehending, and sometimes reluctant to speak of it. With a midwife's help, they can incorporate the experience into their life story.

Many others report nothing out of the ordinary, describing the threshold world as intensely physical, devoid of psychic dimensions. As often as not, they're depressed that Grandmother Nature didn't favor them with a vision. Yet, when they tell their story, the psychic dimension stands out in bold relief. A hawk circled above them every day, screaming something they were too preoccupied to hear. The wind bent them over with the force of truth, but they only felt cold. The lizard doing push-ups in the sun was trying to talk to them, but their thoughts were scattered. The hummingbird buzzed them to say something about jumping as high as they were able, but they were distracted by the heat of the day. With a midwife's help, they can see themselves, their life stories, reflected in the mirror of the wilderness.

Participants in wilderness passage rites must be prepared to enter the threshold with perceptions open to the teachings waiting there. If they are ill-prepared to "get it," then a midwife may have to get it for them. Far better for them to interpret their experiences themselves, than for someone else to perform this service for them. Severance preparation might very well include exercises in sensing the nonordinary, listening to the inner voice, recognizing allegorical or symbolic dimensions, looking for signs and teachings in the natural mirror.

Altered States

Fasting, exposure, and aloneness are ways of "getting high." They illustrate the mind-altering power of taboo, of "going without." In modern American culture, the voluntary exercise of these taboos is almost nonexistent. People unaccustomed to going without may be particularly sensitive and susceptible to altered states induced by their exercise of the taboos. The midwife may be called upon to help initiates navigate a sea of incomprehension, fear, or ecstasy occasioned by alterations in consciousness.

Hallucinations, trances, vivid waking dreams, out-of-body experiences, deep meditative states, "acid flashbacks," psychic states (clairvoyance, clairaudience, telepathy, mediumship), and mystical visions are not uncommon. Sometimes, the experience never actually occurs, but is merely the product of an initiate's desire to be associated with the extraordinary. But at other times, the experience is apparently genuine, a gift in the deepest sense, and a landmark in his search for individuation. It is, of course, important to validate and nurture such gifts in clients who possess them. It is even more important to emphasize that they use these gifts in a balanced way, for the good of their people, dressing their visionary zeal in practical clothes.

The extent to which nature elicits altered states in the human psyche has never been adequately measured. To one who is fasting alone and unshielded, a violent thunderstorm can kindle transitory illusions of threatening or awesome proportions. The steady onslaught of wind or sun can nudge a quester into temporary hysteria or trance. A brilliant, cloudless day can elicit states of "bliss-out" or profound meditation. A dark, moonless night can produce its opposite—blinding inner illumination. But most changes in consciousness are subtle and gradual, evoked by an endless succession of natural images unrelieved by the familiar or civilized. The sense of time slows; internal dialogue grinds to a halt; attention becomes focused or expanded in tune with natural rhythms and forces.

The truth told by an altered state is not always readily understood. Often the meaning of it must be lived out in an otherwise ordinary life. Years ago, a man on a fasting quest experienced a radical shift in consciousness. He was sitting in the darkness when, almost instantaneously, flames erupted around him, burning fiercely before his eyes. He was in a tight, enclosed, boxlike place and was, except for sensations of painlessness, being burned alive. With an act of will, he wrenched himself back into the ordinary darkness of a desert night. But for years after, through the changes of his life, he sought to know the meaning of that experience, even to the point of praying fervently to go back to that place and time once more, to discover the truth of it. Not until the day he committed his mother's body to a crematorium did he realize what the vision meant. He had momentarily experienced the cremation of his own body. "Then I knew it wasn't the hallucination that was so important," he said. "It was the search to know the meaning of it that ennobled my life."

If an initiate has an experience of heightened or nonordinary reality, he often needs help fitting it into the context of his life story. The experience must be interpreted in terms of its relevance to his value system and expectations. It will not do to tell him he should be a medium when, in fact, he is happy being an accountant. Nor does it work to tell a staunch Christian that his vision smacks of the occult or pagan. The most effective tack is to help him find the meaning on his own, without "professional" interpretation. If his life is a voyage of discovery, then it is to his advantage to discover for himself.

It is also important not to exaggerate the importance of visions or altered states. Visions are not ends in themselves. They do not automatically spell change. They are no substitute for honest introspection or the healing expression of emotion, or for the clarity and balance required to give away something of benefit to the people. Visions must be hitched to wagons. Wagons must be pulled.

Visitations and Presences

A woman grieving the death of her husband suddenly became aware of his presence next to her as she sat alone during a vision fast in the South Warner Wilderness. A man alone in his purpose circle in the Funeral Mountains heard a crashing on the slope behind him. In the moonlight he made out the shape of a bighorn ram. The creature with the massive, curling horns approached to within twenty feet of him, stopped, and stood still, looking at him. An adolescent was sitting alone by her fire, celebrating the end of childhood. Suddenly, she turned and saw an old Indian woman sitting opposite her. "Who are you?" the young woman asked. "I'm your grandmother," the old woman said. A woman fasting in the Eureka Valley was drawn to a canyon with a huge boulder at its entrance, and made her power place there. During the night the boulder began to move and change its shape and made moaning sounds. Somehow she endured the night. The next morning she left her fast, declaring she wasn't ready to deal with such power. A man fasting in a canyon in the Inyo Mountains felt something come up behind him during a rainstorm. It grabbed him around the waist, constricting his breathing. An overweight, hypoglycemic woman, fasting in the White Mountains, woke up one morning to find everything, particularly her water bottles, coated with a fur of honeybees. A woman on a passage quest in the White Mountains fell into a soporific fever. At one point, she woke up and looked at the sky. A great, gold-colored bird hovered above her. She wiped her eyes and said, "I must be affected by this fever." But she could not make the bird go away. It hovered above her enigmatically, finally swinging away toward the east.

These are but a sample of the kinds of encounters initiates in the threshold passage are apt to have. Visitations from spirits of the living and the dead, uncanny meetings with animals and spirit creatures, encounters with "allies," aliens, angels, guides, guardians, demons, dragons—reflections of the psyche in the mirror of nature. One finds oneself sorting through such stories, attempting to sift the genuine from the dross, trying not to judge too harshly. To what extent does wish fulfillment fuel visionary action? So-and-so says an eagle landed on his head. Well, that may very well be, but how does that change him? The validity of the vision is directly connected to his ability to find meaning in it, and to incorporate it into his practical life.

In the most potent visitations, there is some form of communication between the initiate and that which appears to him. If he can remember what passed between them, he has taken the first step toward integration. If he can't remember what was said, perhaps he can see or feel what was said. In the absence of a sense of meaningful exchange, the portent of the vision may fade.

Most initiates experience presences or visitations with less intensity than those described above. Perhaps it would be better to say that such experiences almost always occur, but are far less often recognized as such. Only when they appear in exaggerated or heightened form do they sufficiently arouse attention. Hence the old Indian medicine man's vision quest admonition, "Be attentive!" As modern humans are inattentive most of the time, there is little danger that they will overload. Those who enter the threshold half-asleep may not catch the unfolding story reflected in the mirror. We pray that their eyes will be opened to the sacred detail of their passage rite. Those who undertake the rite to flaunt their sacredness, their medicine power, or their divine sanction, need to be reminded of their humanity. For those we fervently pray, not for visitation, but for hard weather.

At the Interface of Natural and Human

The congruence of inner psychological landscape and outer world, of microcosm with macrocosm, of profane with sacred, of human with nature, is typical of experience in the threshing-hold. The initiate's karmic dance in the natural world reflects his inner dance with karma. Of course, this congruence is not just a phenomenon

61

of the sacred world of the passage rite. It happens all the time. But in a passage rite, such congruences, coincidences, and synchronicities are accorded ceremonial attention and significance.

A middle-aged woman, just divorced, "unable to find my place in life," gets lost in the mountains of the threshold. A canyon wren leads her back to her camp. A young man troubled by an uncertain future thinks of his wife, whom he has recently married, and takes heart. He looks up. Two redtail hawks are circling above him. A newly widowed woman sits by her fire and remembers her dead husband. As she starts to weep, coyotes howl in the darkness. A well-educated, scholarly woman, stubbornly refusing to look at her own "shadows," fasts in order to have a "mystical experience." She looks so long into the sun with unshielded eyes that she burns her retinas and temporarily blinds herself. As she gropes about in the pain and gloom, a hummingbird repeatedly buzzes her, confusing her pink sweater for a big flower. A man dances for hours to bring in the spirits. When he returns to his sleeping bag in the wee hours of the morning, he discovers it has been sprayed by a cougar. A young man, determined to have a "shamanic experience," stays up all night in the rain, chanting in his purpose circle. By first light, he falls over, exhausted, and is stung by a scorpion. A man who is afraid of the dark decides to test his courage by taking a night walk. Without mishap he reaches his destination, sits for a moment to rest before heading back to his camp. He hears a scratching, scrabbling sound in the brush behind him. His hair stands on end. He turns to look. It is a baby cottontail rabbit.

In experiences such as these there is a story. The story originates in the mirror of nature, but is written by the initiate. With each person the story differs. But the setting is always the same. The hero is acting out his drama in the natural world. His drama stirs up psycho-physical reverberations, images, and gestures in the mirror. Something in the mirror is aware. Something responds, something that is mutually crafted by natural and human.

In the threshold world, nothing happens by accident. The fallow chaos of the liminal state is given subjective order by the perceptions of the candidate.[3] This order is controlled by the basic tenet that during the ordeal the sacred and profane are one. What happens in the physical world is mirrored in the spiritual, and vice versa. Those who think lightning bolts strike at random ignore the interface of human and nature (of profane and sacred) and fail to see how each is superimposed upon the other. The initiate endures the ordeal in order to know the plan, the design, the symbol, the story that informs his life myth and his giveaway to his people.

Medicine Tracking

In many cases, the initiate must be trained to recognize the signs that he himself has evoked in the mirror of nature. Most civilized folks have difficulty relating to the idea that all natural things leave spiritual tracks, signatures of their sacred origin. During the symbolic death of the threshing-hold, these signatures stand out clearly in the mirror, asking to be identified and claimed. This is evoked by Gary Snyder in his poem, "What You Should Know to Be a Poet." As a poet, he says, you must know:

> all you can about animals as persons
> the names of trees and flowers and weeds.
> names of stars, and the movements of the planets
>   and the moon.
>
> your own six senses, with a watchful and elegant mind.

Truly, the initiate carries a poetic sensibility into the threshold-world. Consider the archetypal connotations of such entities as light, shadow, mountain, sun, shelter, river, spring, desert, forest, meadow, ridge, flower, wind. In the symbolic death of the threshold a child is born who sees the sacral light in everything. Like Adam, he has an opportunity to name everything he touches, to view it in newness of creation. He also has the opportunity to be touched by creation and to be given a name.

Several years ago a twenty-year-old woman came to The School of Lost Borders to participate in an underworld journey for which she had prepared for six months. A month before her journey, she took a medicine walk. A great lover of nature, she walked in a wild place and came upon a deer carcass and antlers. She picked up the antlers. Farther along, she picked up the foreleg bone of some member of the dog species, probably a coyote. She wrote to us, wondering if these signs had anything to do with her "animal medicine." We were noncommittal. What her walk really showed was that she could take care of herself in the wilderness. Perhaps after her journey she would have a better idea what the antler and the bone meant.

During the last days of her preparation time, she pressed the issue again. She'd given the antler away, wondering if that had been the right thing to do. "Ever since I was a kid," she confided, "I wished I had coyote medicine. Think I ought to take the leg bone along for good luck?" We told her to consult an old Paiute healer who lives in our valley. The old man listened to her eager questions, then said, "People don't get coyote medicine until they're over fifty. You've got a long way to go." Then he gave her a searching gaze. "Deer's good medicine," he said. "Deer's good medicine for women."

The next morning we left her at the foot of Crooked Creek in the eastern White Mountains. Seven days, and some twenty miles later, we would meet her at the junction of her canyon and the Bristlecone Pine road, at an elevation of eleven thousand, five hundred feet. Each day of her journey would present her with another ordeal as she climbed five thousand feet toward the top of the range. Resolutely, she turned her back on us, still uncertain what to do about her "animal medicine."

The days passed. We monitored her checkpoints. At Dead Horse Meadow she left a note saying she was OK but the going was rough. Willow and wild rose had impeded her progress up the narrow, trailless canyon. Unexpectedly, she'd encountered fishermen. Not wanting to be seen, she had bounded off through the brush like a deer.

Clear July weather turned sour. Thunderstorms pounded the canyon every afternoon. Flash flood warnings were posted for the White Mountain watershed. Early in the afternoon of the fifth day, her "day of fire," we monitored the checkpoint five miles from the head of the canyon. Another note was waiting: "Doing fine. Tired. Canyon impassable above Dead Horse Meadow for two miles. Thank God for deer trails! Keep expecting to see one." That same afternoon, thunderheads gathered to a blackness around Blanco Mountain and broke into sheets of chill rain. Water in the creek rose half a foot. The night cleared but the temperature dropped.

Only the spirits were watching as she danced all night at ten thousand feet just to keep warm.

With the sixth day, her "day of spirit," came cold, clear skies that quickly clouded. Afternoon brought sleet and wind so chilling she could not face into it and breathe. Later, she related: "It was sometime during this day that I became convinced the deer spirits were helping me. I started talking out loud to them, singing to them to come out of hiding and show me the way." That evening, prompted by a feeling that a large buck with many-pointed antlers was guiding her, she found a small hollow between two overhanging boulders. There she made a dry, warm shelter for the night.

The day of emergence she awoke to a landscape of great beauty. A thin layer of snow blanketed everything. The sun was rising in crisp, clear skies, touching the uplifted monoliths of the Wheeler Crest across the Owens Valley to the west. Awed, she packed up and hiked out the last few miles to the point of emergence. When we did not immediately arrive, she began to reflect. Why hadn't she seen any deer? She turned and there they were, a herd crossing the road, no more than fifty feet away. Moving toward the rising sun, they seemed oblivious to her presence. She counted a dozen fawns and does, and two bucks, one in front, the bigger one in the rear. All at once, the trailing buck stopped and, for a brief eternity, looked directly at her. Then he tossed his many-pointed rack, snorted, and resumed his duties as rear guard.

The story of Morning Deer (as she subsequently called herself) illustrates some of the fine points of "medicine tracking." Genuine medicine empowerment does not come easy. Patience is the watchword. Carefully persevering, the initiate is able to see the stark outlines of his medicine in the mirror of the wilderness:

> Deliberation is one of the qualities of God.
> Throw a dog a bit of something.
> He sniffs to see if he wants it. . . .
> —Rumi, *Mathnawi*, III

Note also how little Morning Deer received from her midwives. The old Indian man gave her a brief opinion, but in no way was she expected to hold to it. The emphasis was placed on her finding out for herself.

Morning Deer completed her first big step toward acquiring "deer medicine." In no sense was her quest complete. She had to return to her people and the demands of a changed life. If deer stayed with her in the years to come, then his power would increase and enrich her life story. If deer was not her medicine, then she would gradually forget, neglecting to pay him honor and respect or to pray for his children. The sound of his inner voice would be drowned by the noise of her everyday life and the roaring of its traffic.

Personal Myth Medicine

A thirty-year-old woman who had been raped at the age of fifteen enrolled in a passage quest course. Twice married and divorced, she confessed that she had come to a crisis in her life. She was contemplating getting married again, but she greatly feared the consequences. The rape had so traumatized her that she had been unable to "let go" sexually with either of her previous husbands. By participating in the rite, she hoped to celebrate once and for all the end of her teenage trauma, to heal this old wound, and to let go of inwardly held anger towards men.

To prepare herself, she went on a medicine walk a few weeks before she began the passage rite itself. When she completed the ceremony, she came to us, told us the story of her walk, and asked us what it meant. Here is her story:

> I took my medicine walk in the rugged San Gabriel Mountains up behind my home. I started at sunrise, with only the contents of my daypack and a jug of water. Because I was afraid of meeting up with some undesirable type, I kept away from trails. It was a hot, clear day. I started sweating so I sat down in the shade of an oak to get cool. A bee started buzzing around me. It was so nosy I finally got back on my feet and started up a canyon. There was a little creek I was walking along, but the brush got so thick I literally had to wade in the creek to make any progress.
>
> Finally I came to the place where the creek came out of the ground. There was a little clearing. I sat down on a rock and looked around. I couldn't go any farther up the canyon. It was

impassable, steep, and tangled with undergrowth. As I sat there in the hot sun, wondering what I was going to do next, I saw the hind legs and tail of a lizard. It had been bitten in two by some predator, maybe a bird. Nearby, I found the front legs and head. For some reason, the severed lizard sickened me. Flies were swarming over the two pieces. I got dizzy and sick to my stomach, and mad that I'd come out there in the first place. . . .

I went back to the spring and sat under a buckeye tree. I thought about John (future husband) at work and wondered if he really loved me as I am, without my act. I imagined him getting tired of me. . . . But that didn't do any good. I drank some water and lay down with my head propped up against the daypack. I think I fell asleep. I had some kind of scary dream that I didn't remember when I woke up.

I lay there for a while, looking up at the sky. Then I got up and went back down the creek, happy to be back in the valley. . . . I sat with my feet in the water for a while, thought about things. I realized I wanted to have a baby with John. Don't know if he's really into it. The creek water cooled my toes. I felt pretty good. I wandered around, looking for something to bring back. I thought about the people at work. What could I bring back to them? For some reason I couldn't get the lizard out of my mind. I wished I was a god so I could fit it back together and make it well. . . .

Just before I started back to the car I found a beautiful bunch of California poppies growing near the trail. First I thought I'd pick just one golden flower. But it seemed a shame to pick one that was in full bloom. So I picked a bud that hadn't flowered yet, and put the stem in my water bottle. That's what I brought back to my people.

Interpretation: The Allegorical Landscape

The initiate is in a double-meaninged universe. Features of the landscape are congruent with an inner, psychological landscape. Ordinary/symbolic, visible/invisible, self/Self are one. What rugged psychological mountains does she hike into? The canyon she chooses is ultimately impassable. Nevertheless, she has to walk up the creek to its source. Why does she have to? Couldn't she have turned back? There's a persistence in her, a determination. But her goal is only to find that she can't go any farther into her mountains of aspiration. The way is too tangled and steep. The route she has chosen takes her only a little beyond the spring.

She discovers the mutilated lizard, empathizes with its plight. The lizard is herself, victim of a predator. Here she finds mute evidence of death, a hint of evil. Her rape trauma is reflected in the mirror of Nature. The sight makes her dizzy and sick; she feels victimized by her own decision to take the medicine walk.

But she doesn't fall helpless under the sway of her feelings. The trauma is old and overgrown with the brush of later experiences. She turns around and goes back to a life-giving source, the spring, where her future husband visits her under a buckeye tree (the bark is still used in veterinary medicine to heal broken-winded horses), and indulges herself by imagining the worst for their relationship. At this point she hits a kind of bottom. The mirror of nature has reminded her of her old trauma and she feels pessimistic about her impending marriage.

The dream—what was the "scary dream?" Was it prompted by the severed lizard? She encountered some kind of monster. Was she defeated or did she vanquish it? The only possible answer lies in her subsequent behavior. She lies there for a while, looking up at the blue sky (the typical medicine color of southwest Indians). Thinking, feeling, imagining what? A meditative state? Whatever, it gave her resolve. She got up and went back down to the valley, where she was happy. Why the valley? What is it about the valley?

Now the pendulum swings toward the positive. She dangles her toes in the cool water, indulging instead of driving herself. Are we, in fact, looking at a way she has of regenerating, a clue as to how she might go about resolving her crisis?

She imagines having a baby with John. She doesn't see his response as being totally negative. There may be some hope. But why should she want to bring a baby into a possibly shaky marriage? Is she going about this the same way she went about going into the steep, forbidding mountains? Step carefully here. Don't push anything. Feel the cool water on the toes. Relax. Think about something else. Find some object that symbolizes what you want to bring back to your people.

As she goes about this search for a symbol of the way to help her people, she entertains fantasies about being God and healing the lizard (that is, herself). All she has to do is fit the rear part to the front part, to join the genitals to the head (or heart).

The golden poppy, the object she finds, is an ancient symbol of sleep and healing. As the myth goes, Demeter, the goddess of fertility, looked a long time for Persephone, her daughter, who had been raped and abducted by the god of the underworld. The gods, taking pity on her ceaseless, desperate searching, caused the poppy to spring up in her footsteps. Whenever she paused to pluck one, it caused her to fall into a healing sleep. Is it possible this woman has been searching like Demeter, desperately, doggedly tracking her violated little girl through the impassable canyons in the rugged mountains? Maybe the gods are saying, "Relax. Healing comes when you release your grip on your pain." The poppy's golden color suggests the rising sun, the promise of rebirth.

She refused to pick a poppy that had already bloomed, preferring the bud not yet opened to the light. Consciously, she chose a thing of promised beauty, of potential splendor, to bring back to her people as a symbol of herself. She earned this positive sign by turning herself away from her wound, as symbolized by the severed lizard. Her entire medicine walk tells a story of a heroine who moves away from the darkness toward the light. Soon she will bloom.

Now she is ready to undertake a passage rite which formalizes the end of the wound's power over her.

Interpretation: Looking for Balance

Every medicine story, such as the one above, reveals important information about the initiate's ability to balance upon the conflicting tides of crisis. A balance between positive and negative elements, for example, indicates a person who is able to go into the darkness and find light, or conversely, one who is able to go into the light without losing his grip on the reality of darkness. The story told only in shades of black indicates a person who may have difficulty regenerating himself. And the story that is told only in shades of sweetness and light indicates a person who is trying very hard to ignore or hide his own darkness. In this woman's story, there is a balance of positive and negative elements. One can confidently assume that, as the years pass, she will move more easily from the trauma of her past into the bloom of her future.

There is another kind of balance to look for, a balance between the child and the adult, between emotion and thought, sensation and understanding, innocence and experience. Does the initiate spend all his time reacting like a child to the outrages of circumstance, or does he tend constantly to filter experience through a rational perspective that does not allow for anger, fear, or tears? If he is "stuck" in one mode or another, the prospects for self-transformation are not so promising:

> Your hand opens and closes and opens and closes.
> If it were always a fist or always stretched open,
> You would be paralyzed.
> —Rumi, *Mathnawi*, III

Interpretation: Making Good Medicine

Reflected in the natural mirror, the medicine story indicates the mode of self-healing. The mode is comprised of the various actions, values, symbols, or archetypes which make up the initiate's "way." The actual healing comes from his being able to accept his "way" as sufficient to his life. His way may not be perfect (whose is?), but it contains inherent gifts and modes of behavior unique to himself. The woman of the medicine story had a tendency to pick impassable canyons, hoping to avoid unpleasant encounters with a monster while following a trail. But she couldn't avoid the inner monster any more than she could avoid the bee that sensed her sweetness. Her means of dealing with the monster, however, was adequate. She turned away from the source of her frustration and pulled herself out of depression with sleep, the cool water of the creek, thoughts of having a baby, and the desire to give something of beauty to her people.

The task of the medicine teacher is to ally himself with Mother Nature, to reflect back to the initiate the acceptability of his way of taking care of himself, of dancing with his monsters, of regenerating himself. The idea is not to point out the flaws, weakness, or inappropriateness of his means, unless, of course, these tools are entirely inadequate. "A physician should be a servant of Nature, and not her enemy; he should be able to guide and direct her in her struggle for life and not throw, by his unreasonable interference, fresh obstacles in the way of recovery" (Paracelsus, *Paragranum*). Nature's therapeutic plan is always the same: to accept, to test, to strengthen, and to teach, regardless of a candidate's relative merits and flaws. Only when he lacks the ability to implement his survival myth does nature show no mercy.

Making good medicine does not mean avoiding the existence of real evil. In the woman's medicine story evil may be found lurking along the trail in the form of a potential rapist and in the mutilated body of the lizard, severed, but never eaten. Emphasis is placed, however, on the initiate's inner resources to deal with the negative forces that threaten her life from within and without. Wherever there is a monster, look for the ways in which the initiate dances with it. Depending on the nature of the monster, appropriate responses run from flight to fight. Usually, it does little good to try to ignore the monster. It will jump out somewhere later on.

In all things, sacred and profane dwell as one. In the threshold-world, shadows, demons, self, and other destructive forces are apprehended in their sacred form. They do not occur at random. Reflected in nature's mirror, they are there for a reason. They are there because the initiate knows (at least unconsciously) that the very thing he fears empowers him and brings out the best, as well as the worst, in him. Hence, negative forces can be allies, personal monsters can be hitched to creative energy. If evil cannot be overcome, at least it can be challenged, encountered, accepted, and changed in the digestive tract of experience. This changed evil can return, as did the unopened poppy, to bloom among the people.

Good medicine, then, has to do with helping the initiate to interpret the meaning of the medicine story for himself, if possible, and helping him to fit it into the context of his life story. With allegorical tools of interpretation, he can accept or transform his means of dancing with negativity, turning his "way" into a healing myth about himself. He can see how his gifts are revealed in and validated by the mirror of Nature. The elder or midwife validates his gifts and helps him to clarify and "own" personal symbols of empowerment and healing, above all, strengthening his ability to read, respond to, and revere the natural order and environment.

The Trickster

Little Mouse jumped as high as he was able and saw the Sacred Mountains. But then he fell back and landed in the Sacred River. He scrambled to the bank, wet and scared. "You have tricked me!" he screamed to the Frog. "Wait," answered Frog. "You are not harmed. Do not let your fear and anger blind you. What did you see?"

Those who are Raccoons at heart are also tricksters. Like Frog, with a perfectly straight face, they can tell Mice to jump as high as they are able. Of course, a Raccoon knows it ain't quite that easy. He's seen 'em come and go. He's seen vision-questing bears get caught in snake holes. He knows little Mouse might fall into a pile of coyote shit, or a pile of his own shit, or a den of rattlesnakes, or a nest of hornets, or a thicket of cholla. In his own indomitable fashion, he'll deal with the "trick." Maybe it'll just be a nice, constant wind, or a thunderstorm, or a sleeping place that never gets soft, or some kind of sickness, or a cloud of mosquitoes, or a pesky rain. Raccoon won't mourn too much for Mouse out there, getting his dunking in the Sacred River. He has to—if he is to emerge as Jumping Mouse.

The ways good medicine can be dispensed via the trickster are too numerous to mention. The passage ordeal itself will turn many an initiate upside down without anyone's help. But occasions will arise. He will come to the midwife, all locked up in self-pity, wildly bemoaning his fate, victimized by the consequences of his own deeds, and blaming it on everybody else. Raccoon might agree with him, lamenting even louder and with such pathos and melodrama that the initiate looks very hard at this passage he says he wants to undertake. A Raccoon might answer another morbidly fearful initiate's twentieth question about rattlesnake danger by replying gravely, "Yes, sir. The desert is crawling with rattlers. No place to stand or sit without smashing one. Don't worry. You'll be safe if you balance perfectly still on the very top of your backpack."

If the candidate refuses to show the child of himself, he can be tricked into fear or anger. If he refuses to be an adult and take responsibility for the childishness of himself, he can be tricked into work, hard work. If he refuses to crawl out of his black hole and see he is made of light, he can be tricked into opening his eyes.

Always, the object of the trickery is the question, "What happened? What did you see, feel, sense, or know?" Was there a dissolving of some limit? Did you go beyond yourself? In the Paiute sweatlodge the "contrary spirit" (trickster) is not "called in" by the interpreter until the temperature in the lodge has reached unbearable heights. When we are all prostrate, gasping for the slightest breath of coolness, at the end of our ropes, then the contrary arrives to announce, "This lodge is so cold it's freezing!" "Let's do something about that," says the old man, who ladles "hot water" on the "frozen stones." With a gut-wrenching hiss, the superheated, dark confinement of the lodge implodes into a kind of hell. Only then can we appreciate the true nature of prayer as the lodge becomes "colder" and we are called upon to sing one more song in honor of the trickster, who teaches us about jumping as high as we are able.

4

Prototypes
of the
Wilderness
Threshold

To this mountain you shall go in a certain night (when it comes) most long and most dark, and see that you prepare yourself by prayer. Insist upon the way that leads to the mountain, but ask not of any man where the way lies: only follow your Guide, who shall offer himself to you, and will meet you in the way. . . . This Guide will bring you to the mountain at midnight, when all things are silent and dark. It is necessary that you arm yourself with a resolute heroic courage, lest you fear those things that will happen, and so fall back. . . .

—Eugenius Philalethes, *Lumen de Lumine*

A wilderness threshold passage takes life, concentrates it into a brief/eternal span of literal/allegorical time, composes a story with a real/symbolic meaning whose mortal/immortal protagonist undergoes an ordeal/epiphany in a bounded/limitless environment where ordinary/nonordinary realities exist simultaneously. The story is both the stuff of action (rite) and contemplation (myth). As the protagonist moves through the plot of the story, he finds himself in a "double-meaninged" universe. An animal is both animal and spirit. A mountain is a mountain and a quest. A star is a star and an angel. A direction walked is a trail and a Way. A dream is a dream and a divine visitation. A mosquito is a pest and a messenger.

The story is always different, depending on the life that is telling it. But no matter how stories differ, there is always a basic, underlying similarity, a kind of archetypal plot or dynamic. This dynamic energizes countless heroic myths, ancient and modern, and stands at the head of Christianity, Buddhism, and many other religions. Joseph Campbell identifies it as the "monomyth."[1]

The monomyth is often phrased as a dragon battle, a dismemberment, a crucifixion, an abduction, a night sea journey, ingestion by a monster, a herculean task, an entombment, a dream or spirit journey, a territorial passage, an ascent of a mountain, or a descent into the underworld. The hero undertakes the trial of the threshold in order to transform himself for the benefit of his people. A king or savior elects to die so that his kingdom may be saved. A goddess descends into the netherworld and is dismembered so that she may ascend again in the spring corn. The hero journeys to the lair of the gods and brings back fire to his people. The Sacred Twins challenge the Gods of Death to a game on the great ball court and outplay them. The Ugly Duckling endures a hard, lonely winter before he inherits his beautiful adulthood. For the sake of love, the fairy-tale princess leaves the protected zone of her childhood castle and enters the dark forest where dwarf tricksters live and witches come knocking with poison apples for sale. Such allegories comprise the archetypal underpinnings of rites of passage and provide a physical-mythical landscape or process within which the candidate lives out his transformation in life station.

Likewise, the modern Mouse leaves everything behind and goes alone to the Sacred River. There he is tried by monsters, often of his own making, and visited by emanations, projections, presences, or spirit guides. Through a long, dark night of the soul, he is rewarded with wisdom, strength, and understanding. He is revived; his inner eyes are opened; a gift is granted. But the main condition of the gift received is that the protagonist must return to the mortal world with his healing vision.

A wilderness threshold quest is "enacted monomyth," or "experienced allegory." The story must be reduced to practical, functional form or process. The plot must be choreographed into a "script," scenario, or drama, and adapted to fit an environment (the wilderness "theater") that suits and enhances the role that the protagonist will play. Every act and scene must glue ordinary (physical) and nonordinary (spiritual) together into a coherent synthesis. The Sufis describe an "interworld," an intermediate kingdom between spirit and body that combines the two into one state of being. The threshold of the wilderness quest is such an interworld.

Prototypes of the Threshold

The work of the midwife is to arrange the various elements of the story into a coherent version of the monomyth that is firmly anchored to both the physical and spiritual worlds: basic plot, setting, duration, characters, and denouement. The story contains elements of trial—thirst, hunger, darkness, isolation, loneliness, exposure, dangerous terrain, poisonous creatures, imagined insanity. This real-life allegory is composed with an eye to balance and symmetry, seeking above all to preserve the material/spiritual, ordinary/nonordinary, mythical/mundane singleness of plot and meaning.

Then the midwife stands back. He has completed one of the most difficult of his tasks—that of implementing an existential scenario which the initiate will now experience as his own life story. The "script maker" must not let this success go to his head or he will surely miss detail that is absolutely important to the initiate's survival of the scenario. The "death" undertaken must always be symbolic.

Models and Model Makers

Monomythic variations of the threshold trial are endless, and relative to cultures. Plot and setting are rendered into myriad different versions of the same theme. Among American Indians, for example, there are countless different wilderness rites, fasting quests, or vision fasts, depending on who is conducting them. Though the Paiute version might differ from the Crow, or the Cheyenne from the Ojibway (or one medicine man's from another of the same tribe), each model is but a variation on the monomyth.

Occasionally, we are aware of claims by "medicine men," or "shamans," (regardless of ethnicity or affiliation) that their model or version of the monomyth is the only true or authentic one. This is like a man boasting that his version of truth is the only version, that all others are false. The wilderness passage rite is not the property of any one nation or tradition. This monomyth is found in the ancestral history of black and white, red and yellow, brown and green.

Perhaps the best and most effective model makers are those who are most loyal to the monomyth itself, who seek to sew fine stitches at the fold of bounded and limitless. They build models they can trust, that will faithfully contain and nurture their "client's" body and spirit. The most trustworthy prototypes are those which have traditionally (and safely) served others. Hence, the effective midwife masters a traditional prototype of the monomyth before he ever begins to experiment with versions of his own creation. The last thing he wants to do is manipulate his charges with a script that contains his own hidden agendas. He knows full well that his charges must find their own agenda, and that his task is to offer a reliable framework within which they may do the finding.

The Ordeal

Because the monomyth always contains an ordeal, the threshold model must contain the element of risk or trial. Without an ordeal, the activity cannot be properly called a rite of passage or initiation. Therefore, a midwife must tread a fine line between severity and safety. He does not want Mouse to be returned feet first. The ordeal must be attuned to the capability of the candidate in such a way as to tax him to the breaking point, but not to destroy or harm him. There are many ways to try him, physically and psychologically, without overdoing it.

The prototypes discussed here are ordeals that primarily involve fasting (without food and sometimes without water), solitude (strict isolation), and exposure to the ways of nature (with only minimal protection). From the perspective of our own work, we consider these essential to the transformational experience. Other kinds of ordeals (fire walking, piercing, flesh sacrifice) are not discussed here—nor are the ordeals we use severe in the extreme (such as ten days without food and water, twenty days in an igloo with only a bear robe, or four days hanging by breast thongs to a tree). Severity or degree of suffering is not always transformational. A "better cure" is not always effected by a "harder trial." Some nuts are tougher to crack, some easier.

Too many midwives err by scorning the rites of passage of others for being "too easy," or not as difficult as what they themselves did. What really seems to matter is the preparation and inner value system of each individual. A villain can undergo a trial and turn out an even meaner villain. "Rake the muck this way, rake the muck that way—it will always be muck" (Martin Buber). All value systems of the world are universal in their condemnation of those who clothe themselves in the rags of righteousness and ceremony, or who mortify their flesh because it serves their pride: "He who walks about naked and lean,/ he who eats only once after a month,/ if he is filled with deceit,/ will be born an endless number of times" (*Sutrakritanga*, I, 2).

The candidate does not undertake the ordeal because he wants to earn a merit badge. He does not need to wear a feather in his hat or a notch on his gun to signify to all that he has passed the test. He bears the signs within his heart and soul. His knowledge of what he has done shines forth from him in the "doing" of his vision, in the newness of his perceptions, in the practice of his "medicine."

Modern Threshold Prototypes

The following models have proved to be effective as "enacted myth" for modern individuals seeking to celebrate their attainment of a new life status. These variations on the monomyth have been put to the test under field conditions. We want to emphasize that none of them are, at the core, the offspring of our own creation. They are traditional prototypes. They have been around for many thousands of years and are extremely effective. Why should we alter a good thing? On the other hand, the manner in which we orchestrate the various elements of the "script" is uniquely our own.

To each prototype we have appended special remarks for those who might wish to implement such wilderness rites among their people. These models are constantly being refined under our own intense scrutiny. The business of building a model takes a lifetime.

Fasting Alone in the Wilderness on the Sacred Mountain

The myths from which this prototype is derived stand at the head of Christianity, Buddhism, and a thousand other religions, including those of many American Indians.

And it came to pass in those days, that Jesus
came from Nazareth of Galilee,
and was baptized of John in Jordan. . . .
   And immediately the Spirit driveth him into the wilderness.
   And he was there in the wilderness forty days, tempted of
   Satan;
and was with the wild beasts; and the angels ministered unto
   him.
—The Gospel of Mark

I took up my abode in the awesome depths of the forest, depths
so awesome that it was reputed that none but the passionless
could venture in without his hair standing on end. When the
cold season brought chill wintry nights, then it was that, in the
dark half of the months when snow was falling, I dwelt by night
in the open air and in the dank thicket by day. But when there
came the last boiling month of summer before the rains, I made
my dwelling under the baking sun by day and in the stifling
thicket by night. Then there flashed on me these verses, never
till then uttered by any:
   Now scorched, now froze, in forest dread, alone,
   naked and fireless, set upon his quest,
   the hermit battles, purity to win.
      —The Buddha, Majjhima-nikava, XII

When he reached the top of the hill, he found that two helpers
had prepared his bed of the sacred sagebrush so that its sweet
aroma rose all about him as he approached, and they also had
placed the five cherry sticks upright in the ground, one at the
center of the highest spot on the hills, and the others all about
four yards away from the center to the four directions. Then
silently they left him, for there was nothing more to do nor to
be said until he came down from his long vigil.
      —Vinson Brown, Voices of the Earth and Sky

The monomyth behind these accounts essentially runs as follows: The time has come for the protagonist to leave his life behind
and go alone to the wilderness, to the Sacred Mountain of vision.
Alone in the solitude and silence, he endures hunger, privation,
loneliness, and the onslaught of the elements in order to earn a

vision for his life and his people. Fasting and praying through a long dark night, he is given a gift, a boon, a sign of divine favor, a spirit guide. When his vigil ends, he returns with power to his people.

Enactment of the Prototype

Usually, the threshold period lasts three or four days and nights. During the time the initiate is alone and fasting, he is allowed water and a few survival items (knife, rope, tarp, sleeping bag, matches, bandanna, jacket, change of clothes, and his journal). He is also equipped with ceremonial tools and certain symbolic items of importance to him. He crosses the threshold alone or in the company of a fellow candidate. If with a buddy, the two will separate at a place equidistant from their respective places, where they will erect a cairn of stones to serve as a checkpoint. Each day at the stonepile they will contact each other, without being seen, thus insuring the well-being of both. If the initiate is alone, he will erect a cairn with the midwife and daily leave a sign there that he is alive and well.

While Mouse is alone in the threshold world, Raccoon watches over him, insuring his safety without being seen or intruding on his sacred time. In case of emergencies, the midwife is available and equipped with proper emergency supplies.[2]

In his threshold solitude, the quester is more or less free to explore his environment. Although some prototypes require him to remain in one place, surrounded by a symbolic circle or edifice, we often find it beneficial to give him room to move and express his desire to seek and find in an outward, bodily way. Of course, safety problems arise with a faster who is free to move. There is always a chance he may get lost, fall off a cliff, or otherwise injure himself. We have accepted this risk if he wants it for the sake of his personal growth. In nearly twenty years, we have not sustained a fatal accident or serious injury. Because the initiate understands and accepts the risk, he tends to act conservatively, mindful of the sanctity of life in his body as he outwardly enacts the personal terms of his quest.

On the other hand, it is also important that the quester spend a good deal of time in one place, within his own private preserve on the body of Mother Earth. At or near his "power place" he will build a circle that orients him to the six directions and represents the circle of his psyche. Within the circle he will hold a wakeful vigil at various times, including the last night of his threshold ordeal.

When three or four days and nights are over, he will recross the threshold and return to the secular world of basecamp, where the midwife waits for him. He will have a story to tell. The story may be interpreted as the story of his life. The protagonist of this life story danced with monsters and trials and other obstacles by virtue of his own vital "stuff" (faith, values, insights, guts). It is up to the midwife to hear this story clearly and to point out its salient features to him (see chapter 3).

Special Considerations

This prototype is particularly effective among youth entering adulthood. Three days and nights alone without food in the track-less wilderness is sufficient for them. Some have protested this is too difficult for civilized young people. But to make it easier would be to water down a time-tested means of identifying and confirming adult sensibilities in the maturing adolescent. Modern youth *are* as capable of enduring this trial as their forebears. A real threshold test elicits the commitment of those who are ready for adulthood. They will not pose a great risk to themselves or others. Those who are not yet ripe will automatically turn away from the apparent diffi-culty of the test.[3]

Adults in life crisis and transition also benefit from this proto-type. Notwithstanding the time spent in preparation (which must be considerable), a week in the wilderness is within reach of most working adults. Part of this week must be spent traveling to and from the wilderness site. Another day can be given to orientation of candidates to the terrain and the rudiments of camping and survival. Another day can be given to incorporation of initiates, before they make the passage to their home world.

Traditionally, many American Indians have utilized similar three or four day and night threshold models. Even today they go to the sacred mountain with little more than a sleeping bag or blanket—and often without water as well as without food. With proper preparation, a modern initiate can go without water for four days, but the risks can be high, particularly with people accustomed to a water-rich life. Those who provide support to a waterless faster should eyeball this person at least twice a day, making certain he refrains from moving around and has shade during the hottest parts of the day. If he begins to vomit uncontrollably or suffer from diarrhea, he should return or be returned to safety. Sufficient moisture may have been lost to warrant emergency treatment. There are other considerations as well. Without water, the body cannot easily rid itself of toxins. A sweatlodge or sauna at the end of the threshold phase will help the faster excrete toxins through his pores.

The Underworld Journey

Mortal existence was often characterized as an underworld journey by cultures as diverse as the Greek, Celtic, Tibetan, Mayan, and Aztec. In an allegorical sense, the protagonist dies and undertakes a spirit journey through the underworld of death to the threshold of birth. As he travels he encounters a series of ordeals which strip away the tattered remnants of his earthly karma and empower him to pass into the "overworld." As he faces the successive trials of the underworld, he sees how the events, personages, and places of his former life are but phantom reflections of his own actions.

Various ritual "instructions" to the spirits of the deceased, regarding the death journey that lies ahead (such as *The Tibetan Book of the Dead*), point out the value of using heightened life experiences to illustrate afterlife states—and vice versa. An Aztec priest annointed the corpse with sacred water and placed certain symbols on the body. As he did so, he chanted: "Lo, with this thou shalt pass the two clashing mountains. . . . With this thou shalt pass the lair of the green lizard. . . . Lo, therewith thou shalt cross the eight deserts. . . . And the eight hills. . . . And behold with what thou canst traverse the place of the winds that drive with obsidian knives."[4] Thus the deceased passed the nine trials of the underworld and came to the place of rebirth.

Similar journeys typify ancient Greek rites of initiation. According to Plutarch, "The Soul [at death] has the same experience as those who are being initiated into great mysteries."[5] Initiatory experiences based on Orpheus-like odysseys are common. Initiates in the Orphic-Pythagorean Brotherhood were expected to memorize the coordinates of the "road to the lower world" before they ever embarked:

Thou shalt find to the left of the House of Hades a spring,
And by the side thereof standing a white cypress.
To this spring approach not near.
But thou shalt find another, from the Lake of Memory,
Cold water flowing forth, and there are guardians before it.
Say, "I am a child of Earth and starry Heaven;
But my race is of Heaven alone. This ye know yourselves.
But I am parched with thirst and I perish. Give me quickly
The cold water flowing from the Lake of Memory."

—*The Funerary Plates*

Odysseus, Orpheus, Hermod (in Norse mythology), Aeneas, and Pilgrim underwent the transformative journey. When the untried Celtic hero Cuchulain resolved to journey to the Isle of Scathath the Amazon to learn the art of warrior craft, he embarked on an underworld passage:

> Cuchulain went on alone, crossing the Plain of Ill-luck, where men's feet stuck fast, while sharp grasses sprang up and cut him, and through the Perilous Glens, full of devouring wild beasts, until he came to the Bridge of the Cliff, which rose on end, till it stood straight up like a ship's mast as soon as anyone put foot on it.
>
> —Squire, *Celtic Myth and Legend*

The heroic protagonist does not undertake this journey for its own sake. He is accompanied by a spirit guide or souls in need of healing. Otherworldly figures visit him as he ventures deeper into what analysts might call the unconscious. He respects these visitations and opens himself to their influences. He emerges with a bright secret burning in his heart. Like birth and death, the "underworld" and the "overworld" are one and the same.

Enactment of the Prototype

There are significant differences between this and the preceding model. The candidate is fasting for a longer period of time (six days and nights), moving alone along a preestablished course in a wilderness place. The distance covered is approximately fifteen miles.

The candidate is given water, a backpack, and certain survival items (knife, rope, tarp, bandanna, sleeping bag, matches, jacket, change of clothes, and emergency first-aid kit). He is also equipped with certain ceremonial tools with which to face the successive trial-stages of his journey.

Of the prototypes discussed in this book, the underworld journey holds the greatest risk. The journeyer must be "buddied" by an unseen person who checks every day (or every other day) on his well-being. This is accomplished by erecting a series of cairns along the route. Whenever he reaches a cairn, he leaves sign of his well-being for his caretaker. Because such cairns cannot easily be found in a trackless wilderness, we select trails or old four-wheel-drive roads as underworld routes. If the candidate follows the route, he can easily reach the cairns where emergency supplies have been stashed. Each night he camps near the cairn, accessible in the event of emergency. Needless to say, the support person must be familiar with the terrain, roads and trails, potential dangers, and water sources of the "underworld" area.

Though the journeyer is fasting, emergency food can be made available at certain cairns along the route. Ordinarily, he will not touch the food, feeling no need for it. A six-day walking fast will not seriously debilitate him. The predominate psychological state will probably be loneliness. The midwife must make certain before-hand that he is emotionally balanced. The biggest risk is getting lost. In the past, underworld journeyers have become lost even when their routes were clear. In every case they were found, or they found themselves, before they got in real trouble.

The initiate may travel at his own rate of speed, provided each evening he arrives at the next cairn. He is bound, however, by the symbolic terms of each day's trial. The ordeals of the underworld journey are seven (counting the seventh morning, when he emerges from the wilderness):

Day One. At dawn, the candidate crosses the threshold of death and enters the underworld alone. At this time he dedicates his journey to the healing of another person and acknowledges that his spirit path is aligned with decision road. The fear of death is the ordeal of the first day.

Day Two. On the second day he does not drink water from one sunrise to the next. Thus he celebrates his freedom from mortal needs. The trial of the second day is thirst for the water of life.

Day Three. On this day he is sealed to the earth. For twenty-four hours he remains in one place and performs a death lodge ceremony. The trial of the third day is the inwardness of entombment.

Day Four. On this day he works to make and sing a spirit song for the good of his people. He fills his lungs with air and sings continually. The trial of the fourth day is the giveaway of breath.

Day Five. The night of the fifth day he builds a small ceremonial fire and feeds it with sticks representing the events and personages of his former life. Then he watches the fire die and keeps an all-night vigil for the coming of dawn. The trial of the fifth day is the divestment of personal karma.

Day Six. On the sixth day he makes the final passage to the place of emergence. The karma of his mortal, underworld existence has been burned away. All that is left is spirit. Hence, he makes himself invisible, so as not to be seen by other humans. He moves around only in darkness. The trial of the sixth day is the spirit passage.

Day Seven. At dawn of the seventh day, he is seen by the guide and takes on the body of his new life. The trial of the seventh day is survival as a human being.

When the traveler emerges from the threshold, several hours must be given to debriefing him. As with other prototypes, the journeyer's story is the story of his life, which, as the ancients saw it, is identical to the story of his final death-passage to new birth. The successive trials withstood represent his innate gifts and abilities to win for himself a useful and meaningful death (birth). The various components of the wilderness through which he passes (the weather, the terrain, the flora and fauna, encounters with people) are to be interpreted as aspects of the physical and psychological "underworld" in which he lives.

Special Considerations

The underworld journey is not an "endurance test." The traveler walks a few miles each day, and on the third does not move at all. Time spent walking is balanced by considerable amounts of freedom. He is free to do nothing, to sleep, to explore, to write in his journal, to meditate. The emphasis is on walking in balance and attunement to the underworld landscape.

This prototype does not preclude chance meetings with strangers. Anyone walking along a road or trail is likely to run across people. The appearance of a stranger may well represent a danger to the traveler. His preparation must include this possibility, however slight it may seem. Some have reported such encounters. A few hid or ran away. Others elected to meet the stranger, considering him to be a potential teacher, guide, spirit, angel, or sign.

Months ahead of time, participants must be oriented to the allegory of the threshold-underworld, and made conversant with the sequence of ordeals and the various opportunities for self-generated ceremony that each day will bring. The above prototype is based on a journey around the wheel of the six directions (see chapter 6). The first day takes place in the east, where birth and death are one. The second day is in the south, where innocence and the senses dwell. The third day is in the west, the place of experience and introspection. The fourth day is in the north, the direction of old age and the giveaway. The fifth day, at the center of the circle, is the earthwardness of mortality. The sixth day, also at the center, is the skywardness of the spirit. The seventh day, emergence, comes back to the east again, to birth/death, at a higher level of awareness.

Underworld journeys do not have to be six days long. Duration varies according to prototype. Setting may also vary, from deep wilderness to rural back roads. Small towns or other features of civilization may be incorporated into the allegorical model. The same holds true for river crossings, passes, campsites, trail signs, private preserves, and other natural features of human significance.

The Earth Lodge

Burial of the dead in the dark, magical soil of Mother Earth is an ancient human custom. At twenty-thousand-year-old burial sites, skeletons have been found curled in the fetal position or aligned with their faces to the rising sun. Archeologists surmise that at a very early time in our history, our ancestors held convictions about the afterlife, regeneration, and the transformation of body into spirit. After the manner of the magical seed, they buried their dead. In the recurrence of spring they saw the return of their loved ones from the netherworld.

The transformational seedtime in the fallow darkness of Mother Earth has been chronicled in many a myth. Jesus was interred for three days and nights in the tomb. Tammuz, Isis, Cybelle, Ishtar, Adonis, Mithra, Attis, Osiris, and Persephone all underwent yearly death, entombment, and resurrection celebrations. These myths are derived from, or are the progenitors of, allegorical rites of passage or initiation where candidates actually descended into the bowels of the earth during their trial. An initiate in the cult of Isis, Apuleius hints about his experience:

> I drew nigh to the confines of death.
> I trod the threshold of Proserpine.
> I was borne through the elements,
> and I returned to the earth again.
> —*Metamorphoses,* XI

The faith of Islam was born in the repeated visits of Mohammad to a dark cave in the desert mountains of Hira. In his womb-tomb the vision finally came:

> The way revelation *(wahy)* first began to come to the Apostle of Allah (Mohammad)—on whom be Allah's blessing and peace—was by means of true dreams which would come like the morning dawn. Then he came to love solitude, so he used to go off to a cave in Hira where he would practice prayers *(tahannuth)* certain nights before returning to his family. Then he would come back to his family and take provisions for

the like number of nights until unexpectedly the truth came to
him.
—*Islam, Muhammad and His Religion*

Even today, many American Indians undertake a vision quest in
a pit, cave, or dark, closed lodge. The quest of Fool's Crow, a
contemporary Teton Sioux medicine chief, is a classic illustration
of the archaic entombment monomyth:

> Stirrup put a black cloth over my head so I could not see where
> they were taking me. Stirrup led the way, and Daniel and Gray
> helped me to walk as we climbed the steep hill. All I had on then
> was a breechclout, and they brought along a blanket, which I
> would use to keep warm at night. When we arrived at the
> questing pit the hood was removed and I saw that it was all
> ready for me. It was about two feet wide, four feet deep, and
> six feet long. Sage had been spread on the bottom to purify the
> pit and to make a bed. I jumped into the pit, and following
> Stirrup's instructions, I lay down with my head toward the
> west. Then the men stretched a buffalo hide over the pit, pegged
> it down tight, and left me there alone.
>
> I stayed in the dark and damp pit for four days and four
> nights without food or water. On the fourth day I woke up and
> discovered that the buffalo robe had mysteriously and silently
> disappeared.
>
> —Thomas Mails, *Fools Crow*

Note that Fool's Crow does not dwell on events that transpired
while he lay in the darkness of the pit, nor does he speak of his
discomfort. On the fourth day he had a vision. The tomb covering
disappeared. Through the vanished seal he emerged on the fifth
morning. In his heart he held the secret so ardently sought by
medieval alchemists:

> He who makes everything descend from heaven to earth, and
> then ascend from earth to heaven, has information about the
> Philosopher's Stone.
> —Vallis Novi, *The Hermetic and Alchemical Figures*

The monomythic challenge of the Earth Lodge runs as follows:
Summer has fled. Now the leaves are changing into the bright

colors of fall. Obeying an inner longing that cannot be denied, the protagonist leaves the rest of the world behind and crawls into a dark, secret place in the earth to die and be reborn. He fills the emptiness of this small place with his body, as the dry hulk of a seed surrounds the precious spirit within. He covers himself with night and allows the silence to possess his earthen bones. In the womb-tomb of the Great Mother, time is called "wait." Sound is called breath, stomach, or heart. Vision is a dark screen illumined by whatever the protagonist dreams or paints there. With nothing to eat, drink, or do, he pays close attention to his inner darkness. His dry mouth fills with cotton; his belly cries for food; his body gets so cramped and pained that he almost has to forget its existence. He cannot endure this dark passage of waiting without learning the secrets of surrender. When the yielding comes, the dry husk of his spirit seed splits apart. He is no longer a prisoner of himself or his circumstances.

His spirit breaks forth from its bed. The dying place is opened. Dawn floods the emptiness of the earthen tomb. Where is the initiate? He is not here. He is risen newborn into the world.

Enactment of the Prototype

The lodge itself may take various forms, depending on location and available materials. Ours is a water-hollowed limestone hole five feet deep and six feet in circumference. During the daylight hours, the opening is covered without sealing off the air supply. There are many other kinds of Earth Lodges—predug pits, natural caves, prospect holes, barrows, sweatlodges. A small edifice with opaque walls, like a miniature sweatlodge, can be built, with willow or birch ribs covered with canvas, blankets, vegetation, or earth. Provisions must always be made for a slight but constant flow of fresh air. This can be done without letting in light. There must be enough room in the lodge for the candidate to lie at full length and to turn over.

The candidate is brought to the lodge at sunrise, often at the conclusion of a sweatlodge, sauna, or ritual bathing ceremony. The lodge has been furnished with beneficial herbs and a bed of rushes, grass, or sage, and purified with the smoke of a sacred herb. If he goes in naked, then a blanket or sleeping bag must go in with him. Except for personal symbolic items, he enters bereft of all civilized comforts, with the possible exception of a container for urine. (A bowel movement should be taken before entry).

He stays there for two or three days and nights. Forty-eight hours is usually sufficient for a modern person. Buried in his seed chamber, he sleeps by day and stays awake by night. During wakeful hours, he sings, chants, cries, converses with himself or others, or prays for what lies deepest in his heart—or he is silent. He cries for a spirit or power song and grapples with his whirling mind. Dreams and apparitions may appear. Time passes slowly.

The midwife stays nearby the entire time the initiate is entombed. At sunrise and sunset he removes the flaps over the entrance and speaks briefly to his charge. This is the time to find out how he is doing and impart words of cheer. Such exchanges should be kept short. There will be time for talking later. Then the covering is resealed and the initiate is again enshrouded in darkness.

At sunrise of the third or fourth morning the lodge is opened and the person comes forth. In most cases he does so under his own steam, emerging into the blinding light of dawn.

An appropriate incorporation ceremony should be held when the long vigil is ended. A sweatlodge, sauna, or ritual bathing is called for. Traditionally, food (and often water) is withheld from the candidate until the sweatlodge is complete. Then a great feast is held for his benefit. On the day following the feast, the initiate is thoroughly debriefed.

The total "inwardness" of the Earth Lodge is unique and psychologically productive. The candidate's experience focuses on his mental and emotional states. Boredom and physical discomfort are major themes. Boredom is not inert and dead, but fallow and chaotic. Within the fallow darkness lie the patterns and themes of his threshing-hold "story." Though he may be inclined to think that nothing happened while he was in the lodge, he can be helped to see what monsters, guiding spirits, or illuminations came to him while he lay in the darkness. As the days of his incorporation pass, his understanding will grow. He will come to look upon his experience in the darkness as regenerating or visionary.

Special Considerations

The initiate can be helped to prepare by being taught how to sense intuitively and explore his "inner story" as it unwinds nonstop from the reel of his consciousness. Useful tools are self-guided fantasies, hypnagogic meditation, mantras, chants, songs, and the like. He can help himself by being specific about why he is undertaking this ordeal. He can use this reason as a kind of litany, singing it to himself when times are hard.

Physical and dietary preparations for going without food and water for forty-eight hours or longer require an increase in fluid and food intake for at least two weeks before the trial. Indian medicine teachers and our own experience convince us of the advisability of starting a food and water fast with a full belly. A well fed and watered modern person can usually go three days and nights in a sun-shielded place without great difficulty.

Those who steadfastly refuse to look within themselves, to accept responsibility for what they have done, or to accept the necessity of change in their lives can profit from even a single hour spent in the earth lodge—if someone stands watch, prays, and helps them to understand what happens to and through them while they are alone looking into the dark mirror of nature. In some traditions, the dark earth lodge is where a man may find the woman of himself *(anima)* and the woman, the man *(animus)*.

Other Prototypes

The prototypes discussed here may be altered or redesigned. A four-day-and-night fast on the mountain can be shortened to twenty-four hours and still be of therapeutic benefit to participants, particularly to young people aged ten and over. The six-day underworld journey can be shortened or lengthened according to the midwife's design. What is found here merely reflects our own unique practice, just as the particular sweatlodge ceremony performed by an Indian healer reflects not only a tradition or mythology but also his particular and personal methodology. The midwife will find his own myths, allegories, and prototypes. He will devise his own allegorical/real frameworks within which others can make their own medicine. There is one all-important stipulation. Under no circumstances should a midwife ask a person to undergo a threshold ordeal that he has not personally experienced.

There are many other threshold prototypes, not discussed here, that use the constants of fasting, exposure, isolation, and a natural setting. Peak ascents, all-night walks, marathons, river runs, tracking expeditions, canyon ascents and descents, cross-country ski tours, and many other experiences can be transformed into allegorical threshing-holds, particularly when the other two phases (severance and incorporation) are duly formalized. Outdoor experience schools such as Outward Bound and National Outdoor Leadership Training Schools have recently begun to see the value of consciously exploring the metaphorical dimensions of their course experiences.[6]

Any design must be mindful of the midwife's own heritage, of the voice of his sacred ancestors dwelling in him. We would advise against adopting *in toto* someone else's prototype unless one has been well trained by that person to conduct the model impeccably. This advice is especially true of American Indian models. It would not do for a white person never apprenticed to an Indian to be so presumptuous as to copy a traditional Indian model without transforming that model within the alembic of his cultural milieu and life perspective. Of course, there will always be underlying monomythic similarities among all models within a given genre.

Any initiatory threshold prototype must be approached with fear and trembling and conduct proper to a professional. Not only must the midwife know his model well (having learned it by experience), but he must also know people well. One shouldn't even think of taking up this work without being trained (or acquiring comparable experience) in both wilderness ways and the ways of human beings. Accustomed to human frailty, one must also be accustomed to one's own frailties, and must not fall into the ego-pride trap that begins to insist that "my model is the *only* model." No one has a right to his model if he cannot respect the models of others.

Ethics of Apprenticeship

I hold the earth to be sacred, inviolable, a living entity to whom I owe my very life and death. I respect, protect, and conserve her, leaving as little trace as possible of my sojourn, or passage through, the wilderness. I teach others to do the same.

I am well trained, experienced in the various aspects of my profession, having acquired the skills, credentials, and personal mastery of the true professional, seeking always the safety and well-being of those I serve, doing nothing to harm their physical, emotional, mental, and spiritual health.

I use pancultural or traditional forms, allegories, prototypes, teachings, and ceremonial ways that are appropriate to the life goals of the individuals I serve. I respect the unity in cultural diversity, honoring in the monomyth, humanity's common roots. I heed the inner voices of my own ancestral heritage, heeding also the wisdom of many races, cultures, and colors.

I construct and maintain safe prototypes within which individuals may mark the end of life transitions or personal crises, providing a beneficial means by which they may incorporate their wilderness passage into a new life purpose or station.

I do not allow others to undertake any ordeal, test, or rite that I myself have not personally experienced.

I network, in good will, with others in my profession, and honor and respect our differences as well as our similarities.

5

Rites of the
Wilderness
Passage

Rites . . . together with the mythologies that support them, constitute the second womb, the matrix of the postnatal gestation of the placental Homo sapiens.
—Joseph Campbell, *The Hero with a Thousand Faces*

It all comes down to a single moment in the life of each Mouse. He stands alone at the gates of the sacred threshold. Before him lie the features of eternity. By his own efforts he has become a worthy candidate. Now the cord binding him to his former life must be severed. He will cut the cord by entering the passage. This is an auspicious and powerful moment.

At first, the absence of civilized things within the field of perception creates a huge emptiness, around which the conditioned self flutters like a doomed moth. The quester sets up little projects, civilized ways to pass the time. His mind races through all the old ruts he thought he had left behind. He keeps thinking something will happen, something unusual or otherworldly. But the hours pass without incident. The feelings of emptiness deepen. He wonders, "If this is a sacred world, where's the magic?" He compares himself to the great heroes of the quest and comes up wanting. "I am not worthy," he thinks. "God has not chosen me. God will not send an angel down to wrestle with me. I am alone and forsaken by all."

Eventually, he will be forced to pay attention to the features of eternity. His ego will begin to seek other forms of nourishment. Without food, company, entertainment, or (as in the Earth Lodge) light to see by, he must rearrange perceptual priorities and look for different cues to occupy his attention. His mind will forage deeper for sustenance. Small things will begin to arrest his eye. He will spend more time looking off into space. He will begin to feel what the silence is composed of: the varnish of stones, the loom of cliffs, the bareness of ridges, the scat of small animals, the flatness of the dust, the sighing of the evening star, the luminosity of darkness.

Generally he will sink into less ordinary states. He will begin to feel the connection between himself and all human creatures. He will "know" his relationship to the natural world of his place, not as an individual, but as Everyman. He will look down at his hands and feet and feel their connection to the earth. He will think thoughts and feel emotions that seem to flow through him like a great river. He will start to walk with the gait of his sacred ancestors.

He may also become aware of sounds, but from what source? He will hear voices, yet not see another living soul. He will listen closely, if only because he has nothing better to do. The voices will teach him that in the threshold-world, past, present, and future are one in Now. As he listens he will shed his sense of impatience. It will not matter that the sun seems to stand still, or that he is running out of things to do. He will feel eternity in the sounds that break the silence: the beating of his heart, the rumble of his stomach, the whistle of air in his nostrils, the wind in the trees, the drone of a fly, the distant roar of a jet plane, the scratching of little rat feet in the sand.

Then, perhaps, Everyman will become aware that something is watching him, aware of him. Spooked, he will look around. Dark earth, blue sky, vegetation, birds . . . what could be watching him? Everything seems so unconcerned. Yet the feeling is unmistakable. There is an Awareness that is aware of him. He wonders if he can communicate with this Awareness. "Yes, yes!" urge the sacred ancestors in his blood. "There are ways to communicate. Perform ceremony."

The Function of Threshold Ceremony

Maintenance of the relationship between "natural" and "human" (as in the term "human nature") is a basic function of threshold ceremony. Mother Nature needs the ceremonies of humans if she is to reveal her sacred face to them: "Nature needs man for what no angel can perform on it, namely, its hallowing" (Martin Buber).[1] Delores La Chapelle hypothesizes that ceremony activates the lower and midbrain powers of perception, thus enabling us to communicate with animals, rocks, and other spirits that inhabit natural locales: "By such rituals, the human being can get in touch with the information accumulated through millions of years of evolution of the human brain."[2] The ceremonies of the quester demonstrate this hypothesis. Human beings can and do communicate with other creatures, entities, and spirits on profound levels of understanding. As one quester put it, "It's as though there were a high priest or priestess in us all."

When a human communes with Mother Nature, she communes with him. She blesses his way by balancing his steps, by keeping him alert and healthy in her graces. She guards him from falling: "And those who love their Mother, she never deserts them. As the hen protects her chickens, as the lioness her cubs, as the mother her newborn babe, so does the Earthly Mother protect the Son of Man from all danger and all evils" (*The Essene Gospel of John*).[3] Through performance of ceremony, the quester determines and sacralizes his deepest myths about himself. His actions forge the connection to his place on the earth.

Traditional Symbols and Ceremonies of the Wilderness Threshold

The following can be read as a list of ceremonial tools or "devices" which various traditions have employed during the threshold phase. The ritual material may enhance Mouse's perception of his threshold experience. Of course, he is free to do what he wants with this information. If he choses to use it, he will be drawing on the ancient power of the archetype to inform and transform his psyche, for each device is a window, a chink in the cavern through which the infinite is perceived, a ceremonial means of poising the body-mind in sacred space, of centering the human heart in sacred time.

The Threshold

Ramon bent down and laid his bow and arrows crosswise over his shaman's basket—bow and quiver pointing east in the direction of Wirikuta *[sacred mountains of the Huichol]. He rose and conducted what appeared to be an urgent dialogue with unseen supernaturals all the while gesturing with his* muvieri *[shaman's feathers] in the direction of the world quarters and the sacred center.*

Visually, the passage through the clashing cloud gates was undramatic. Ramon stepped forward, lifted the bow, and placing one end against his mouth while rhythmically beating the string with an arrow, walked straight ahead. . . .

—Peter T. Furst, *Flesh of the Gods*

An invisible door stands before the quester. Beyond the door, deity abides in the wild garden-womb of nature. The seeker is now at the limits of his ego, the boundaries of its influence. He must step beyond his former limitations and enter this region of magnified power. He must venture beyond the "protected zone" of civilized life and nakedly inherit the forces from which a secure life has shielded him. To an unprepared initiate, the dangers of the threshold are legion. If he fears too much or trusts too little, the world he enters will be as a darkened screen against which unconscious fears will be freely projected. Monsters of his imagination will swallow him up. "The adventure is always and everywhere a passage beyond the known into the unknown; the powers that watch at the boundary are dangerous; to deal with them is risky; yet for anyone with competence and courage the danger fades" (Joseph Campbell).[4]

The threshold crossing is celebrated by building a symbolic representation of the gate, threshold, or boundary: gateposts, pillars, or a passageway, which the initiate traverses. The crossing requires a formal dedication or invocation, calling on the help of unseen witnesses, spirits, directional powers, or God, and is a time to make an offering. The ceremony is concluded when the initiate steps through the opening into the embrace of the sacred world. The gateway must then be dismantled and any sign of the crossing erased. It will not do for negative influences from his former life to follow him in.

He may want to linger more than a moment at the portals and

remember, before he goes any farther, that he has come here to die symbolically. He might feel eager and impatient, but if he waits and consciously checks himself, he will cross the threshold with focused intent when, finally, he cuts the last thread and steps beyond the zone of protection.

The Lost Soul

One day a man passing through a wood heard a raven calling.
When he was near enough, the raven said: "I am a princess by
birth, and I am bewitched, but you can deliver me from the spell."
"What must I do?" asked the man.
"Go farther into the wood," said she.
—The Brothers Grimm, "The Raven"

One of the names for the passage quest is "healing journey." The quester undertakes to heal himself *and* his people. Among traditional cultures, shamans and medicine people embarked on interior or netherworld journeys to gain secrets to the healing of sick patients. The hero-savior Jesus undertook a death passage so that his people could be saved. The sun undertakes a dark journey so that the lost earth will be found at dawn.

If he wants to carry the spirit of a "lost" or sick companion with him on his threshold journey, the quester must not do so because he is determined to heal a wretch less fortunate than he. Such charitable impulses are not heart-deep. The erstwhile healer will forget about his charge halfway through the trial. There must be a deeper connection between the candidate and the lost soul, a feeling that the healer cannot make it through the trial without the support of the one who is to be healed.

A person formally dedicates his trial to a lost soul just before he crosses the threshold. He clearly visualizes and addresses the one to be healed, stating his healing intentions, and asking for permission to carry them out. The lost soul must be entrusted to the care of powers higher than the journeyer. A symbol of the lost soul is affixed to the candidate's clothing and is not removed until the threshold journey is complete.

Healing is imparted via the candidate's threshold adventures. In a figurative sense, the lost soul suffers the same trials as the quester, and receives the same benefits. The healer's medicine is transferred to the sick one. This transference is based on the profound notion that we cannot heal others unless we heal ourselves. Conversely, we cannot heal ourselves unless those around us are in need of healing. Deep in the healer's heart, the healer and the one to be healed are one.

The Power Place

The only way to get to know this country (any country), the only way, is with your body. On foot. Best of all—after scrambling to a high place—on your rump. Pick out a good spot and sit there, not moving, for a year. Keep your eyeballs peeled and just sit there, through the hours, through the days, through the nights, through the seasons—the freeze of winter, the stunning glare and heat of summer, the grace and glory of the spring and fall—and watch what happens. Pick your place and stay there. You will become a god.
—Edward Abbey, *Beyond the Wall*

Initiates often wonder how they will go about finding their fasting place in the wilderness. They look up at the great mountains and wonder where in all that vastness their special nook lies. They stand on the brink of decisions that are symbolic of how they find their place in the wilderness of their lives. Raccoon's role is not to tell them what to do. He need only offer advice pertinent to their survival and then stand back and watch them act out their own place-finding stories.

Years ago, a seventeen-year-old girl returned early from her fast, claiming she had not been able to find her place. Unhappy with the spot she had originally chosen, she had wandered for two days in a kind of numbness, frantically looking for *the* place. When night fell, she put her sleeping bag down anywhere and slept in the fear that she did not belong to the ground upon which she lay. After counseling, she saw what had happened. Her inability to find her place reflected the rootlessness of her life, having been shunted back and forth between divorced parents and grandparents from an early age. Her attitude toward her body also reflected her sense of homelessness. She hardly lived there. Since the age of thirteen she had ravaged it with addicting drugs. Without a worldly, or a bodily, home, her spirit wandered aimlessly, exposed and afraid.

The power place always expresses something unique about the psychic landscape of the candidate. Some choose the tops of mountains, others canyons or caves. Some delight in ridges, others in trees. Some are drawn to water, others to barrenness. Some want soft sand, others are attracted to hard ground. We prefer to see the "power place" as a place within the quester himself (as well as a specific geographical location), a focus of power which recognizes the mirror of itself in the surroundings.

A person looking for a power place must keep certain survival considerations in mind. Will it be a safe place in a lightning storm? Is it prone to flash floods? Does it offer adequate protection in the worst weather? Where will he sleep? If he needs to, can he put up a tarp there? What kind of scars will his occupancy make on the environment? Is it a safe place to build a fire? He cannot be babysat. He must make the choice and live with the consequences of finding his place in life.

Once he thinks he has found the place, he spends time there to make sure he has not been misled by his enthusiasm or impatience. He lies down upon the earth of his place to sleep or dream or otherwise surrender himself to influences of the locale. Permission is requested from the spirits or powers in the form of an offering or prayer. It is very important for him to feel that he has the permission of those whose land he is occupying—the native souls who linger there. Invariably, there is a sign that the place is or is not the special purchase he seeks.

A place of power is powerful if the initiate considers it to be so. A candidate's decision must not be objected to unless it holds unusual survival hazards. The judgment that some places on the earth are more sacred or more powerful than others is purely subjective, relative to the perceptions of each candidate. Nevertheless, for him it is truth, and truth carries the power of transformation. We have great respect for this kind of knowing, for we too have our own private places of power in the wilderness, and we go to them whenever we need an infusion of their élan. One area is on the top of a great mountain. The other is a seemingly insignificant dry wash near the bottom of a desert valley. High or low, distinctive or humble, every inch of the earth is sacred.

> I came to my place and I put down my pack. I took one of the sticks I had brought—my "snake stick"—from the mesquite spring on the way here. It was in my left hand. I knew I had to make an Invocation to my place. I stood at the center of the ancient stone circle, facing east, then west, then north, then south. . . . When I was finished [with the invocation] I wept, standing in the circle. Then I put the water jugs in the shade. I spoke to the spaces in the rockpile where I intended to build my shelter. I said:
> "Snake, I have come to spend three days and three nights in this spot. If you are here, speak now."
> Then I poked all the holes with my stick. There was no rattle. Then I drank three swallows of my water, spilled three swallows into the ground at the center of the depression, and drank the rest.
>
> —A Quester, aged fifty-nine

The Fast

For I tell you truly, except you fast, you shall never be freed from the power of Satan and from all diseases that come from Satan. Fast and pray fervently, seeking the power of the living God for your healing. While you fast, eschew the Sons of Men and seek our Earthly Mother's angels, for he that seeks shall find.

Seek the fresh air of the forest and of the fields, and there in the midst of them shall you find the angels of air. Put off your shoes and your clothing and suffer the angel of air to embrace all your body. Then breathe

106

long and deeply, that the angel of air shall cast out of your body all uncleannesses which defiled it without and within.

—Jesus, in *The Essene Gospel of John*

As a ceremonial medium, fasting is one of the oldest and finest. In a world of civilized convenience, it has fallen somewhat from favor, for it involves self-denial. Still, the ceremony has not lost its power. There are emotional, metaphysical, and spiritual dimensions to it, known to our ancestors, which invite discussion.

Fasting is like cultivating the soil so a seed may be planted. The body is stirred and emptied so that the spirit may grow in it. Fasting nudges the body up against an instinctive fear of death, foreshadowing the ultimate emptiness. The candidate makes an agreement with fear: "I will allow you to fill my emptiness—so that I and my people may live more fully."

A wilderness fast alters the civilized consciousness. The psyche is open to orchestration by the elements and rhythms of the natural order. The environment rushes into the vacuum in the pit of the stomach. The senses begin to eat in unaccustomed ways. Eyes devour, the nose tastes, the mouth smells, the ears ingest. Sunrise is meat and noon is wine. The dark wind sets a banquet. The inward landscape also changes, is rendered more vivid and terrifying. The seemingly trivial becomes momentous; the forgotten is dramatically remembered; the vague assumes clarity and immediacy. Perceptions sift the important from the unrelated and accentuate dreams, reflections, fantasies, and intuitions. Self-transformation becomes possible.

Without ballast in his belly, the initiate begins to understand what it means to "walk in balance on the Earth Mother" (Sun Bear)—compensating for loss of strength by applying weight of spirit. He steps carefully, economically, in harmony with the terrain. He loses any desire he might have had to run down a scree slope or climb a twenty-foot dry waterfall. He does not venture too far from his place. He paces himself. Not under pressure to get anywhere, he has time to pause, examine, and communicate with size, shape, color, function, and species: a hunk of pitted limestone, a city of kangaroo rat holes, a poppy blossom, a strand of cholla, a furry ant, a smooth stretch of quartz sand, a flake of obsidian, rabbit tracks, a wild bee hive, a belly flower, a rock stained with bird shit, the drone of a fly, a methodical stink beetle, a skittering lizard, a bunch of native grass, a moth flutter, a weathered sagebrush root, a garden of stones. He walks amid this bounty and measures all with fast-induced myths and values. He learns to follow his nose, to trust his own way of composing an itinerary, of charting his "life map."

When he stops to rest, he has nothing to put into his body but water (sometimes not even that). He cannot sit down with the evening paper and some munchies to enjoy the view from his terrace. All he has is the view. Because he has nothing else to eat, he eats the view. He hears his empty belly gnawing on the silence. A cool breeze on a hot day stimulates his taste buds to salivate. He experiences the avid emptiness of his body turning inward on itself for food. The shadow of death falls across his path, quickening his heartbeat, pumping him with a strange lethargy. His body is reduced to imitating the animal hunger for life that exists in everything around him. Even as the toxins exit his body, his civilized veneer begins to crack. Contradictory emotions, sensations, feelings flow into the breach. He notices the way he occupies space, the signs and marks he leaves behind: his urine stain on a rock, his bootprints in the sand, broken twigs. "Nature" is no longer an abstract notion, no more a romantic ideal, but a real, whole, living entity. He sees clearly that he has no desire to harm or befoul her, or even to leave signs of his passing.

The midwife also knows what it is like to fast. He respects the candidate for what he is doing. He knows that many times the faster will feel exhausted, lost, and abandoned by all, his spirit lying prostrate at the throne of mercy. He knows how the faster will be praying with dry lips and a gaunt belly. As night falls many will sit down to dinner, their perceptions clouded by conversation and full stomachs. But Mouse will be sitting on a ledge, hungry and alone, watching the stars appear one by one.

Note: Certain precautionary measures must be taken with candidates who, for medical reasons, might injure themselves with a prolonged fast. Pregnant women, diabetics, and certain kinds of hypoglycemics are among those who may need to take a little food along.

The Stonepile

While wandering about the desert one occasionally encounters piles or mounds of rocks that have every appearance of being arranged by hand. . . . as with petroglyphs, there have been many speculations about the purpose of these mounds; they are frequently called "Indian Post Offices."
—Emory Strong, *Stone Age in the Great Basin*

The heaping of stones is an ancient practice, a symbolic act of communication, a mute affirmation: *This is the way. This is the meeting place. Borders touch here. Someone lies buried here. Peace to all who pass.* The stonepiles we find in the desert are said to be as much as ten thousand years old. They bear little resemblance to "white man's stonepiles," which usually take the form of large boundary or lode markers. "Indian Post Offices" are modest and inconspicuous, blending with the environment, easily overlooked by anyone who does not know they are there.

The cairns constructed by fasting "buddies" for safety purposes are small, like their native counterparts. But they are not permanent structures. Having served their lifesaving purpose, they will be removed when the passage is done. They are erected at the borders of power places in prominent, easily found locations. During the threshold trial, they are visited each day by questers who leave signs for each other or their midwives that they are all right. If a quester does not leave a sign at the stonepile, his buddy or the midwife must go and find out why he did not carry out this response-ability. It may be that the quester is injured, sick, or otherwise incapacitated.

The modest little cairn is a monument erected in the name of human love. There have been times of emergency when this simple stone heap did, in fact, save someone from harm. The link that holds us together, that enables us to survive, is fragile and precious. Though we are unique and alone, yet our destiny is common and the earth is shared among us and all living things. We must care for those linked with us. Without them we would not live another day.

The Dream

*The water bug is drawing the shadows of evening
toward him across the water.*

—*Yuma Indian*

Initiates cross the threshold with high hopes for a "dream vision."
But many return claiming their dreams have failed them. They say
they did not dream at all, or that they only dreamed about common,
ordinary events in their lives. They must be reminded that whatever dreams they have *are* important (even the ones they cannot
remember having), even as the everyday events of their lives are
important. The vision lurks somewhere—in the kitchen sink, in the
bedroom, in the attic.

Sometimes threshold dreams are singularly clear and powerful.
Within them the dreamer finds a name, a story, or a life mission.
Sometimes the dreams are ambiguous and confusing, like a maze,
seemingly involving the dreams of other dreamers. Sometimes the
dreams are personal and emotionally demanding, awakening the
dreamer with tears. Sometimes, the dreams surface only vaguely,
disturbingly, in the waking mind. Sometimes the dreams come and
go like tides, subtly wreaking their changes on the shores of consciousness. Many times the dreams come when the dreamer's eyes
are wide open. Daydreams, woolgatherings, waking fantasies, and
hallucinations are not to be discounted, for they are also water from
Oracle River.

There are a large number of techniques used in dream counseling
that will serve any midwife-therapist well. We are partial to Jungian metaphors, to the notion that the dreamer's collective-uncon-
scious "dream oracle" yields the dream so that the dreamer can
integrate it. For the ancestral oracle is very wise and seeks to aid
the dreamer to grow into the fullest dream enactment of his place
on the earth. Like an aeolian harp, the oracle is sensitive to the wind
shadows that pervade the dreamer's psyche as he moves through his
environment. It trembles to consciousness as the water bug draws
the shadows of evening into the center of his skittering dance.

The Oracle is aware that the dreamer has entered the sacred
threshold. No details are irrelevant. Unfortunately, many candi-

dates have a tendency to forget the details, for one reason or another, or can only remember scattered fragments. They must be encouraged to write down their dreams in journals.

Even as our bodies require water for survival, so our spirits drink from the river of dreams in order to survive whole. Dreams are unawakened acts. The candidate must be able to examine them in the light of conscious, meaningful action.

The Sacred Fire

Defenseless under the night
Our world in stupor lies;
Yet, dotted everywhere,
Ironic points of light
Flash out wherever the Just
Exchange their messages:
May I, composed like them
Of Eros and of dust,
Beleaguered by the same
Negation and despair,
Show an affirming flame.
—W. H. Auden, "September 1, 1939"

As a symbol, force, element, spirit, god or goddess, fire has been a fundamental symbol in the world's mythologies. It has also played a major role in countless traditional ceremonies, including wilderness passage quests. Many initiates plan ceremonies around a sacred fire, but all too often lack fire-building know-how and must be instructed in the use and meaning of a small fire that leaves no recognizable scar. Instruction is best carried out in the field, where all the requisite materials exist. As an instructor demonstrates the ignition, maintenance, and disposal of a fire, he can also discuss fire symbolism and its many applications.

The initiate must be clear about why he wants to build a fire. If he just wants to take the chill off his bones, he will be wasting wood that belongs to and sustains the flora and fauna of a sacred place.

If he plans a specific ceremony with fire as the central symbol, then his modest, carefully laid fire will burn brightly and teach him many things. But he must take pains over how and where he builds the fire. In most national parks and monuments, campfires are not permitted except in designated areas. National forests and wildernesses also have regulations, including fire permits. Fires must not be built when fire danger is high.

The building of an ecologically sound fire is itself a ceremony. The fire pit should be no more than six inches deep and a foot in diameter, scooped out by hand in a spacious area of sand or soft dirt free of ignitable vegetation. Roots should not protrude into the pit. Pits must not be dug on desert pavement, fragile meadowlands, alpine sedge, thick chaparal, pine-needle cover, or any other delicate surface. The completed firepit is ringed with spark-arresting stones. The fuel is gathered from widely scattered locations. It should only be dead and down wood. Only a small armload of twigs is needed. The fire will last no more than a few hours.

When darkness has fallen, the carefully laid tinder is ignited with a wooden match. As the flame reaches up it is fed with wood that represents the flesh and bones of the quester's life. Twig by twig he gives himself, the persons, events, and symbols of his past to the warm light of his oxidizing life. With the last twig, death-darkness envelops him. The coals grow black and cold. When the fire has sunk into complete darkness, his former life has ended.

All sign of the fire must be erased. The coals must be cold and mixed with the same dirt that was scooped out. The ring stones are scattered unobtrusively over a wide area. If it is godlike to make a fire, it is equally godlike to make a fire disappear.

In Mayan mythology, the gods created the earth (and the universe) five times. The fifth and last creation was beautiful—but it was static. Nothing moved. The sun hung motionless. The planets stood fixed in their courses. Things did not grow. Everything looked ripe and good, but it was barren. The gods conferred among themselves and decided that in order to give motion and life to their creation, one of their number would have to be thrown into the fire of the sun. All were afraid to die. Finally, Xipe Totec, or "No Skin," volunteered to jump into the sun. The ugliest of the gods, he had been born without a skin. Like a flaying victim, his uncovered flesh clung to his bones. He threw himself into the sun and immediately everything began to move. Time started. All things in the universe began to enact the rhythms of birth, copulation, and death. Xipe Totec, the martyred "No Skin," was reborn as the patron of spring—the god of flowers.[5]

The seasons turn on the cosmic wheel of fire. The laughing boy of summer matures, bears fruit, and declines in the fall, wasting away into winter, the "Skinless One." In the dead of winter, when everything is barren and still, old age jumps into the fire of spring. The infant god of flowers is born. Winter sacrifices itself for spring. Fire is the passageway between them. Forever it must feed on the dead and give forth the light of life. The spark that leaves the corpse aches for the tinder of a new body. Always Prometheus will shake his fist at the death-minded gods. There *will* be fire!

The Gift of a Name

Jacob was left alone. And a man wrestled with him until the break of dawn.

When he saw that he had not prevailed against him, he wrenched Jacob's hip at its socket, so that the socket of his hip was strained as he wrestled with him.

Then he said, "Let me go, for dawn is breaking." But he answered, "I will not let you go unless you bless me."

Said the other, "What is your name?" He replied, "Jacob."

Said he, "Your name shall no longer be Jacob, but Israel, for you have striven with beings divine and human, and have prevailed."

—Genesis 32: 25–29 *The Torah*

The initiate often returns from the threshold with the gift of a "medicine name" that identifies the essence of his powers or abilities. He has wrestled with the spirits and has prevailed. Now, like the lame Israel, he must live with the consequences of his name.

During his time alone, the quester will seek such a name, for he will be surrounded by a million metaphors all suggested by the wild body of Mother Earth. He can best help himself by keeping his senses and mind open. He will find that a true name is not attained without doggedly seeking for it. For his name, Jacob wrestled all night with an angel. A quester may very well need to do the same.

A good rule of thumb is the idea that the name itself is related to the way in which the initite seeks it. Hyemeyohsts Storm tells a fable about how a young man obtained his medicine name. A "Young Man of the People" went to his grandfather and said:

> "Grandfather, I hear that somewhere there Exists a Singing Stone, and that when it is Found, it will Hold great Medicine for its Finder. Is this True?"
>
> "It is True," answered the Grandfather. "Go to the North and you will Find it."

So the young man went north, seeking the Singing Stone. After many adventures, he arrived in the north and found his grandfather sitting upon a stone, waiting for him. "The Singing Stone is not to the North," said the Grandfather. "It is to the South." So the young man journeyed south, and after many adventures, he found a dragonfly. "The Singing Stone is not to the South," sang the dragonfly. "It is to the West." So the young man journeyed west and found a mouse. "I am seeking the Singing Stone," he told the mouse. The mouse answered, "The Singing Stone is not to the West, it is to the East." So the young man journeyed east, and after many adventures he arrived at a strange camp. He headed toward the camp but pulled up short when he saw that the paintings and signs on the lodges were foreign. He decided to go ahead, in spite of the "Bow of Tension Pulled within Him." Finally, he reached the circle of lodges. "Then his Sisters, Mothers, Brothers, Fathers, Grandmothers, Grandfathers, Uncles, Aunts, and all his Relatives Came Out to Greet him, saying, "Welcome to our Counsel Fire, Singing Stone!"[6]

The search itself earns and confers the name. The seeker becomes what he has been seeking. The search is both outward, through the physical events of his life, and inward, through terrain of thought, emotions, dream, and revelation. Which direction to seek? Every direction. The name does not come until the search is complete, until the angel has been wrestled with.

The initiate must not be afraid to travel in realms where language breaks down and becomes anachronistic, where all maps, signs, and roads are foreign. Grandmother Nature does not communicate in one's native language. Her names for him are found in wind and storm, cloud and sky, creature and creation. If he perceives these things with the conditioned eyes of civilization, and pigeonholes them with labels or nomenclature, he will never attain the secret name-magic he seeks. A hawk will call his name and he will not hear because he thinks he is just looking at a hawk. An ant will tell him his name and he will ignore what it says because he thinks he is just watching an ant. His inability to recognize a messenger from the Great Mother will be a sign he is not ready to find what he is looking for.

The true power of a medicine name lies in its secrecy. The more he keeps the name to himself (especially when he is tempted not to), the bigger the name will grow in him. As the power of the name grows, so he will grow. The name will sprout within him and bear fruit for all to see. But if he should broadcast his name to all and sundry, the name may slip away. He will begin to imagine that others are judging him critically for not living up to the name and he will wish he had never told them. The name will become a burden rather than a gift and be quickly forgotten.

It is common for a person to return from the threshold without a name. He may be disappointed, particularly if he sought long and hard in a careful, focused manner. Apparently he has some distance to cover before the name inheritance is his. The power of his name, once he finds it, will be correspondingly greater because he will have given so much of himself to the search.

Meeting Strangers

"Everyone Genero finds on his way to Ixtlan is only an ephemeral being," don Juan explained. "Take you, for instance. You are a phantom. Your feelings and your eagerness are those of people. That's why he says

115

that he encounters only phantoms on his journey to Ixtlan."

I suddenly realized that don Genero's journey was a metaphor.

"Your journey to Ixtlan is not real then," I said.

"It is real!" don Genero interjected. "The travelers are not real."

—Carlos Castaneda, *Journey to Ixtlan*

Occasionally, during his time of threshold isolation, a quester will encounter a stranger. The possibility may frighten him. Women especially, for good reason, have shared this fear with us. Though such meetings are rare, the possibility cannot be ruled out totally, no matter how carefully a midwife has gone about ensuring privacy for his charges.

Encounters with strangers, benign or malevolent, during a passage quest or spirit journey, has been a part of the ceremonial drama of wilderness rites for thousands of years. Among the aborigines of Australia, people on spirit quests followed the tracks of mythical heroes through legendary regions, crossing tribal and religious boundaries, meeting strangers and groups of strangers who played significant roles in the allegorical unfoldment of the quester's life story. Likewise, pilgrims and supplicants of countless followings have traveled to holy shrines or sacred places and have run into foreigners or aliens—ghosts, spirits, angels, messengers, and even gods and goddesses in human form. Usually these strangers are benevolent; sometimes they are bent on mayhem.

Traditionally, a stranger possesses mana, or personal "medicine power." Consider the impact of a stranger's intrusion into the purity of an initiate's wilderness solitude. This impact is a measure of the mana of the stranger—a power potentially dangerous unless rendered harmless through certain actions collectively called "rites of incorporation with strangers" that are designed to disarm the "evil eye," to render the quester free of the "conditional curse" placed on him by the presence of the stranger.[7] Note the word *incorporation*. When meeting strangers, it is important to "take on the body"—that is, to become corporeal. The traveler must not only get back into his body, but he must also see that the stranger takes bodily form, too, for then he can be properly perceived and dealt with.

An adapted version of "rites of incorporation with strangers" has often been a part of our preparation of underworld travelers. This formal procedure comprises a step-by-step series of actions intended to render a stranger neutral or benevolent (see below). It is used only if the traveler has been seen by the stranger. If it happens the other way around, the traveler can elect to melt into the landscape and become invisible.

1. Stop. If you are seen, and you run, you may incite predatory instincts in the stranger. He may become curious. He may pursue you for altruistic reasons, thinking you are in some kind of trouble. There is also a good possibility the stranger is a benevolent or guiding spirit.

Stop, compose yourself, become strong in the circle of your purpose. Remind yourself that you are on a quest. What you are doing is powerful medicine to the stranger. Stop and hold your ground so that the stranger can feel your mana.

2. Wait. Hold back before you move. Assume a neutral appearance—relaxed, grounded, yet swift to flee if threatened. Invoke the help of your gods and powers. Examine the manner of the stranger. Feel his presence. Can you guess what he is doing out here in the middle of nowhere? You are fast approaching a decision whether to remain or to exit. If the stranger feels uncomfortable or looks awkwardly connected to his body or to the ground, remove your presence by turning away casually, without signs of panic, and walk into the surrounding cover. Once out of sight, put distance between yourself and the other. But if you chose to remain, take the next step.

3. Go Through. There is a threshold here that must be crossed consciously. You make an effort to close the space between your circle and the stranger's circle. You move toward the stranger whether or not he moves toward you. As you cross the boundary, prepare yourself to accept the karma of your decision to meet him.

4. *Enter.* Enter the region of the stranger's personal power, imposing your circle on his. Enter as neutral or benevolent, a real person, solid of foot and self-contained. Make no attempt to be anyone other than who you are. Remember that you have made the decision to meet, and that therefore the stranger is at least provisionally under the influence of your mana. Examine what kind of queer fish you have caught in your net.

5. *Be Incorporated.* Fully own your body by interacting with the stranger in the "here and now" of conversation. Why is he in this place? Where is he going? Does he require anything of you? Do you require anything of him? Whatever is said between you will cling to you after the encounter is over. Do not invent stories about your situation. Traditionally, the powers protect a person on a spirit quest. Observe the stranger closely. Is he who he says he is? Or is there something about him that does not ring true? At any time you can begin to withdraw yourself subtly from his presence.

Benevolence must be met with good will. But do not go anywhere with the stranger. Remind yourself that you are "in transit" and that only you know the real direction you must travel. This stranger is a "karmic ghost" created by your decision to enter the threshold.

6. *Sever.* Parting must be decisive and friendly. Remember that you are disengaging your circle from that of the stranger. Leave nothing important of yourself behind in his possession. Redirect your attention to the path ahead and do not dwell nostalgically on the meeting. Sever cleanly and completely.

7. *Go Back Through.* Now widen the space between your circle and the stranger's. As the distance increases, you will begin to "dis-incorporate." Now, instead of suggesting the intention to meet, you are suggesting your intention to leave—by *not stopping to look back.*

8. *Dis-Incorporate.* When you can no longer be seen by the stranger, you are "invisible" again. Now you can rest for a moment and shake the dust of the encounter from your circle of purpose. To make a formal end, smudge yourself with the smoke of an herb,

wash your hands, or just take a deep breath and give thanks. Your full attention must be redirected to the path ahead. If the stranger was an "angel unaware" or a spirit teacher, you will discover the purpose of his visit as you go along.

Menstruation

When a woman at the "dark of the moon" is disturbed by a sense of disharmony in herself, irritability, inertia, or restlessness, she may be able, by deliberately taking time to be alone, to gain a unity of psychological aim within herself, which the primitive woman found, perhaps, through submitting to the imposed taboo. A period of introversion and seclusion of this kind is often very valuable, but it must be a real introversion, a turning within, *more actively undertaken than a mere submission to physical necessity.*

—M. Esther Harding, *Women's Mysteries*

The everyday life of a modern woman floats upon the surface of a deep, rhythmical flow determined by the phases of the moon. Like her sacred ancestors, she cannot ignore these rhythms. But unlike them, she does not celebrate the onset of her menses by removing herself from normal life and human contacts. She goes on with what she has to do and is most likely to see her "period" as a slight bother or discomfort. Rationally, she no longer subscribes to the ancient taboos regarding the "uncleanness," "curse," or "corruption" of her body during her menses. But she has forgotten that her sacred great-grandmothers had good reasons for going into seclusion at this time—and good reasons for supporting mens' superstitious fear that women in their moon were an evil influence and that they should be excluded from village and family life until they were "clean" again.

Most American Indian women gladly accepted menstrual restrictions: "Women did not usually think of menstrual taboos as a

119

burden, but as a way to get out of daily chores and thus a welcome rest. Life for most Indian women was no less hard than that of the men, but they were given little prestige and honor. They were glad to be left alone."[8] Feminist anthropologists have recently suggested that women themselves were responsible for the imposition of menstrual taboos—including women's rites of isolation, purification, and first menses. Because these rites existed, "primitive" women enjoyed a privilege that modern women do without—a kind of spirit passage every month.[9] It would indeed be unfortunate if modern women completely lost their deep, intimate connection to Mother Earth and to their sacred great-grandmothers' moon-cycle ceremonies.

During her threshold trial, a seventeen-year-old faster wrote in her journal: "Damn! Lightning and thunder! Looks like it's going to rain. Guess what? My period came! It wasn't supposed to come for another week. Now what am I going to do? Cramps. No tampax. I'm so scared and lonely. God, I wish I was back home!" Her experience is typical of many women whose periods have come ahead of schedule (or on time) during the time of aloneness and fasting. Rather than regarding its arrival as a misfortune, the initiate can be encouraged to view it as an opportunity to celebrate the mystery of her body and her membership in the sisterhood of all women. At the "darkening of the moon" women have tradition-ally been imbued with an excess of power, making them "danger-ous" to be around. Fortunately, her period has come during the threshold time, while she is alone and can look within to watch, listen, and feel. If a dark thing is in her heart, she can bring the adversary out into the open, using her "moon power" to reconcile oppositions and confusions within herself. She may want to per-form a ceremony enacting her relationship to earth and sky, moon and water, allowing the influences of the darkness and night to wash her clean, even as the blood of birthing returns her seed to the earth. She can offer her menstrual blood to the earth in grati-tude for the mystery of her fertility.

A woman in her moon can be "set apart" from the rest of a group by making everyone aware that she is in her time. She need not be segregated in any other way. Aware that everyone is aware, she will appreciate the significance of her condition. She might watch her interactions with men during this time, for many men still retain a deep-seated fear of a woman in her moon. Males can be reminded that their bodies and psyches are subject to tides similar to those that rise and fall in women, and encouraged to explore the relationship between their emotions and the moon.

The Purpose Circle

God is an intelligent sphere whose center is everywhere and whose circumference is nowhere.
—Hermetic Axiom

The purpose circle or "circle of the self" is customarily built some time prior to the last night of the threshold period in an area that has been selected with great care. The circle is not made carelessly or halfheartedly, for it symbolizes the initiate's relationship to the universe. Usually, it is composed of stones, each selected for shape, color, size, or "feel." Each stone represents a loved one, teacher, animal totem, spirit, directional power, persona of the self, or other entity that comprises the invisible circle of his life purpose. There is no rule regarding number of stones or circle design—both should be of significance to the quester. The idea is not to cram a bunch of material together to make a crude symbol, but rather to construct a "living," proportioned, personally meaningful picture of the invisible circle of a life purpose.

Before it is built, the circle can be aligned with the six directions. When the cardinal points are laid down, the rest of the circle can be filled in. It should not be too large in size. We suggest making it a little too small in diameter to lie fully outstretched. That way, the seeker cannot go to sleep so easily. He must also take notice of the kind of surface on which he is building his circle. If the ground is as fragile and delicate as desert pavement or alpine sedge, an all-night dance or a ceaseless pacing around the circle will not do here. He must chose a place that will bear his marks more fleetingly.

When finally arranged into a finished design, the stones will encircle the center as the body surrounds the heart, forming a protective enclosure, a "circle of immunity," a "ring pass not," a spherical interface of awareness between self and universe that is mutually integrative, reciprocal, and healing. When the builder's

121

patient work is done, he may decide to consecrate his circle with prayers, offerings, songs, and so on, remembering to thank the spirits of the place for allowing him to make his "last stand" there.

Just before sundown, he stows all his gear except what he intends to take into the circle with him. He needs little—his sleeping bag, some water, possibly a personal symbol, music-maker, or journal. As it grows dark, he enters the circle. He removes one of the stones, as though he were opening a door, and steps into the circle. Replacing the stone, he closes the door, and seals self inside Self. He will remain there until the disk of the sun strikes the opening of his earthen tomb.

The moments before entering the purpose circle are particularly moving if he imagines he is living the last night of his life. The long, usually undramatic hours of the vigil are thus enhanced and enlivened. He sees more clearly what is important or not important to his life story. He resists sleep because he wants to find out what it is like to die. Though his death is only metaphorical and imaginary, it generates a secret power afterward, a self-knowing in him. He has sat on a mountain all through the night and entertained the most powerful ally of all—his own death. Now he has some "death medicine."

> Great Spirit,
> when we face the sunset
> when we come singing
> the last song, may it be
> without shame, singing
> "it is finished in beauty,
> it is finished in beauty!"
> —Evelyn Eaton, *The Snowy Earth Comes Gliding*

He stays awake through the long night hours, conducting himself within this sacred "circle of the self" as he sees fit. Sometimes he paces between the cardinal points and cries to the powers of direction for a vision. Sometimes he uses the circle to integrate and balance himself. Sometimes he dances clockwise around the circle all night, singing his calling song. Sometimes he sits quietly in the center and peers into the darkness, waiting for a sign. Sometimes, he falls asleep in spite of himself, only to awaken later to rueful fears that he has ruined everything by dropping off. The predawn hours may find him bleary-eyed and groggy from lack of sleep, barely clinging to wakefulness. He will be rewarded by the almost imperceptible quickening of dawn.

"Nothing happened in my purpose circle," complained one returnee. "Do you mean the crickets didn't sing; the wind didn't blow through you; the moon and stars didn't flow across the sky like a great river; you had no emotions or thoughts?" we inquired. "Oh *that*, " he laughed. "I guess I was looking for something special." Looking for "something special," we miss the vision of what is already there. Truly, a great deal happens while the hero is in his circle. All of it together composes a story of how he sat up through the night and sought a vision for his people. The theme goes: "This is how the person creates meaning for himself." You might want to ask him about this story when he returns from the threshold.

The fact is, by the time he steps out of his purpose circle, something has happened, whether he is aware of it or not: "Forces will have been set in motion beyond the reckoning of the senses. Sequences of events from the corners of the world will draw gradually together, and miracles of coincidence bring the inevitable to pass. . . ." (Joseph Campbell).[10] When he comes forth from his circle, he is the naked kernel, free at last, his shell dissolved in the currents of the Sacred River. The soil in which his fetal spirit roots is the dawn light of his incorporation.

Crying for a Vision

As the hart panteth after the water brooks, so panteth my heart after thee, O God.

My soul thirsteth for God, for the living God: when shall I come and appear before God?

My tears have been my meat day and night, while they continually say unto me, "Where is thy God?"
—Psalm 42: 1–3

Black Elk referred to the threshold of the vision quest as the *hanble-cheyapi*, or "lament for a vision." In a noble ceremony the "lamenter" staked out a six-directions circle and walked back and forth between each cardinal point and the center, crying, "O Great Spirit, be merciful to me, that my people may live."[11] This traditional cry contains the secret of the visionary prayer. The seeker does not go down to the Sacred River merely to fast and pray for himself. If he brings nothing into his purpose circle to take back for the good of his people, he has no reason to be asking in the first place.

The entire threshold trial can be spent praying, crying, lamenting, supplicating, singing, chanting, imploring, invoking, beseeching, or calling upon the powers that be. Though there is no standardized means of addressing God, each person must be comfortable with his own way. Some have claimed that they do not know how to pray. Some are embarrassed, claiming the subject is "unscientific." Others are bitter, saying, "My prayers have never been answered." It always helps to explore the person's conception of prayer and himself as pray-er.

When he is alone, he will pray as he sees fit. No one will be there to applaud his piety. He does not need words. Appropriate prayers for feelings deeper than words are literal cries, unadorned, unformulated, unhindered by any tradition. As he lies in the dust like any wretch, waiting for death, the cry that goes out from him expresses his deepest longing to complete himself and his world. May he cry for loneliness, for love and caring, for helplessness, for fear and doubt. May he cry as long and loud and hard as he needs to. No one ever said the healing quest was painless or polite.

Crying or praying for a vision does not mean trying to have faith that the Great Spirit will descend in a flying saucer or otherwise mystically validate the petition. Signs of an answer will be part and parcel of the lamenter's ability to see into the mirror of nature. From this experiential framework will come insights, inspiration, self-awareness, self-empowerment, a personal *mythos*, inner resolve, dreams, spiritual revitalization, groundedness, love for Mother Earth, or self-transformation. All of these are components of vision. All of these are answers to the classic cry, "Be merciful to me, that my people may live."

After all these things and near the daybreak there shall be a great calm, and you shall see the Day Star arise and the dawning will appear, and you shall perceive a great treasure. The chiefest thing in it, and the most perfect, is a certain exalted tincture, with which the world . . . might be tinged and turned into most pure gold.

—Eugenius Philalethes, *Lumen de Lumine*

During the all-night vigil in his purpose circle, the initiate will symbolically pass through the "contraction field" surrounding his own birthing. His singing, crying, dreaming, feeling, even his attempts to keep himself awake, comprise the birth contractions. With the first finger-touch of dawn light, birth is imminent. Soon his questing spirit will recross the threshold and be enveloped in the body of the "profane world." He will emerge newly born into a world of experience, no longer the "initiate," but the "initiated."

The first light is often called "false dawn." But even the feeble light of an unrisen sun dispels the gloom of night. Objects and features emerge into clarity and color. But direct sunlight is still an hour away. Through gritty eyes he looks out on an imperceptibly brightening world stirring to life with bird song and insect chorus. He shivers in the gray light and chafes at the bit. The last mile is the hardest. Now he must play the trickster game of false dawn. It says, "I'm going to trick you into thinking that this morning, of all mornings, the sun will not rise unless you do something to bring it up."

The newborn child comes into the world singing. The quester may want to do the same. Or he may find some other way to bring the sun into the world, for if he does not make it rise, he may abort his own birthing. His head crowns the thighs of Mother Earth. As she pushes, he comes forth by his own effort, singing in gratitude for her mercy bestowed on him. Then he must decisively cut the cord connecting him to his power place, the placenta that has nourished his gestation.

The stones of the purpose circle must be removed and scattered unobtrusively. He may want to leave the cardinal points intact. Later, when he returns to this place, the four stones will mark the circle's exact location. Once this is done, he expresses ceremonially his gratitude to the earth and the spirits of the place for his safekeeping and gives the rest of his precious water to the life there. He sterilizes the torn ends of the umbilical cord by meticulously erasing any obvious sign of his stay. This is not a time for nostalgia, but for resolution. He cannot consider his trial to be over. It has just begun. He puts on his pack and says goodbye to his place. Then he walks away. "Having departed from your house, turn not back; or the furies will be your attendants" (Pythagoras).

When he recrosses the threshold, enters the people-boundary, and other eyes again view him, he will possess a body, a personality, a self-consciousness, a circle of purpose, and a vision. He may feel reluctant to return. This reluctance is a form of self-indulgence. He must face the life he has inherited by the right of his passage. He must vacate this zone of magic and descend into the circle of the familiar village. The time has come to embrace the return cheerfully, to look forward to the challenge of bodily existence.

No matter how sensitive or exposed he may feel in the dawn moments of his incorporation, it is a given of his life that he now walks among people and assumes the necessary ego-survival behaviors. Birth emergence requires a loss of freedom. Now he must contend with gravity. God has to become mortal; Self must become self; spirit must descend into ego-body. In time, he may remember his threshold trial as a moment in eternity—compared to the swamps in which he is currently mired. Should this not be an indication to him of how he might fondly remember his life some day, when he stands at the actual threshold of death, when the roaring of the Sacred River in his ears is like thunder?

Be careful at completion as you were at the beginning.
—Tao-te Ching, 64

6

The Six
Directions
of the
Threshold
World

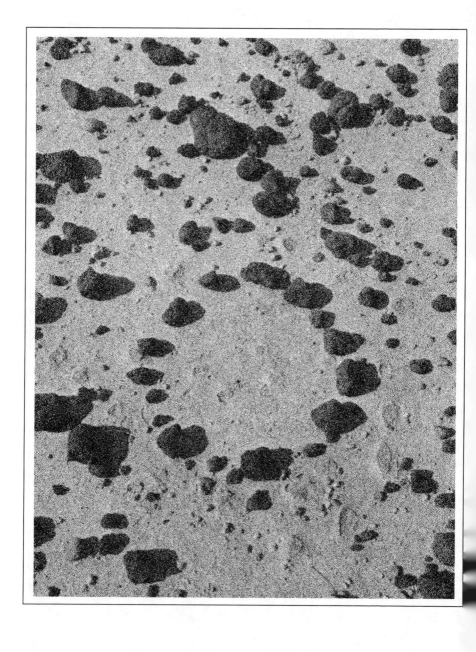

*The four directions plus upward and downward
constitute the spatial continuum (yu). What has
gone by in the past and what is to come in the
future constitute the temporal continuum (chou).
The universe (these continua) is mind, and my
mind is the universe. Sages appeared tens of
thousands of generations ago. They shared this
mind; they shared this principle. Sages will appear tens
of thousands of generations to come. They will share
this mind; they will share this principle. Over the four
seas sages appear. They share this mind; they share this
principle.*

—Lu Hsiang-Shan, 1139–1193

Any discussion of the six ceremonial directions of the wilderness threshold begins with the circle. "There is much power in the circle," said Black Elk. "Birds know this for they fly in a circle and build their homes in the form of a circle; this the coyotes know also, for they live in round holes in the ground."[1] The old chief was emphasizing the importance of this symbol in the ceremonies of his people. Within the sacred time-space circumference of the circle the Oglala Sioux performed the *wiwanyag wachipi* (sun dance), *inipi* (sweatlodge), and *hanblecheyapi* ("crying for a vision" or "vision quest").

As Black Elk implied, the circle shape is prefigured throughout the universe, from the realms of the subatomic to the interstellar, in an endless variety of entities, forms, and formulae. From our earlier history, the human race has traced and ceremonialized this shape. Recognized from infancy, the circle is the simplest yet the most sophisticated of human symbols: "The circle or sphere is a symbol of the Self. It expresses the totality of the psyche in all its aspects, including the relationship between man and the whole of nature" (Jung).[2]

Of all the symbolic constructs related to the wilderness fasting quest, the circle is the most prominent. All other rites and symbols are subordinate to its convergent meaning. The initiate builds a circle ("purpose circle") of stones, at the center of which his highest purposes are focused and his tiny life oriented to the vast universe. Therefore, he must be prepared to use this symbol to its fullest advantage. Severance teaching must include six-directions circle lore.

The Circle of the Self

To follow the meaning of the six directions as the ancients plotted them, you begin by drawing a circle around yourself. Then you stand in the center of the circle and face the direction in which the sun rises. Place a marker at the eastward edge of your circle. Then turn and face the opposite direction, westward, where the sun sets. Place a marker there. Draw a line between the two markers, defining an east–west axis. Now turn ninety degrees and face northward toward the constellation of the Great Bear and its fixed polestar. Place another marker at the northern rim. Then turn around and face the opposite direction, south. Place a marker on the southern rim and draw a straight line between the north and south markers. Now your circle is quartered. Where the two lines cross at the center is your place in the circle.

Now pick up the circle and hold it around you like a hoop. You have added two more directions: downward and upward. This turns your circle into a ball or gyroscope. Imagine your circle suspended around, above and below you. Walk around with it. Notice that as you move, the circle stays fixed, compasslike, on the six directions. You, at the center of your circle, move, change directions, and revolve through the points of the compass. No matter where you wander across the face of Mother Earth, these directions will remain constant. The ancients called these directions "powers" or "spirits" and endowed them with symbols, ceremonies, and names, claiming that the powers existed within and without their bodies.

The distinction between what is inside the circle and what is outside, between self and Self, is a necessary illusion shared by all humans. The distinction is drawn because we must survive in a physical world. Nevertheless, the inside and the outside are (and are not) one and the same. The "knower" and the "known" are (and are not) one and the same:

> Whatever being comes to be,
> Be it motionless or moving,
> Derives its being from the union
> Of "field" and "Knower of the
> field"—this know.
> —*Bhagavad-gita*, XIII, 26

As he sits in his wilderness purpose circle, Mouse must realize that within his tiny rodent breast dwells the timeless, omnipotent agency often identified as Self. He may attempt to fool himself into thinking he is looking out through mouse eyes. But immortal Self is also looking out and seeing a great number of little selves. Altogether, these little selves compose a symphony of Self. A fundamental objective of the purpose circle is to acquaint the little self in the purpose circle with the great Self within and without.

Self also encloses and surrounds self. The six directional powers of Self are pinions holding the circle steady. They are points of balance, like the feathers of a hawk soaring in tricky winds. The six-directions circle attaches the self to Self. And in an opposite but equally true sense, the directions bond the Self to self.

But enough of this heady discussion. The six-directions circle is not simply a transpersonal construct, a philosophical system, a geometrical or mathematical formula. It cannot be statistically measured or quantified. It is, however, a process, a natural design, a perceptual framework. It is most like a mandala poem. It involves the whole being—the light side (east) and the dark side (west), the emotional plane (south) and the mental plane (north), the profane (earthward) and the sacred (skyward). In a way, the six directions are a story that is told both episodically and all at once. The directions are like stepping-stones; yet all directions are found in any one stone.

Obviously, one does not undertake the study of the six directions from an exclusively rational perspective. By the same token, one is equally incapacitated when approaching it from a solely emotional, phenomenological, or imaginative perspective. Our discussion of the six directions, then, will mingle the poetic (east) and psychological (west), the sensational (south) and the intellectual (north), the gross (earthward) and the refined (skyward). We will anchor the circle of our purpose to the six directions, and thereby connect these words of self to the Heart of Self.

The Six Directions

What is presented here is a synthesis of teachings received from others, enriched by our own perceptions.* This material is not given as dogma or doctrine, but as a blank canvas on which the colors and images of an archetypal mandala poem bloom suggestively. This is not a picture of Reality, but a picture of how Reality might be perceived. The reader will soon note the subjective nature of some of the directional designations. Unabashedly, we include the fact that we were born and raised in a Judeo-Christian culture and that a desert environment comprises our local flora and fauna.

We begin our discussion in the south, with the powers of childhood and innocence. We might have begun in the east, with the powers of birth. But we prefer to start with the naive trust of the south, with the understanding of the child. Our metaphor of growth will move clockwise around the rim of the circle, as the sun moves across the rim of the earth. Eventually, we will come to the east, where the aged child of the south will be born.

Those familiar with the crises and transitions of human growth may wonder how long it takes for an individual to grow through the six directions. A lifetime? The mandala poem cannot be ensnared in a temporal net. Though it is obviously linked to the seasonal cycles (summer-south, fall-west, winter-north, and spring-east) and to the major passages of life (childhood-south, adulthood-west, old age–north, and death/birth–east), the cyclical, spiraling growth curve of the six directions is also profoundly rooted in the dynamics of human transformation (severance-south, threshold-west, incorporation-north, and enlightenment-east). It is also related to the constant, almost instant-by-instant adaption to changes in environmental stimuli (reaction-south, internalization-west, orientation-north, and realization-east). An initiate's threshold story

*Others include Hyemeyohsts Storm, Rocky Storm, Stephanie, Swift Deer, Sunwater, Evelyn Eaton, Sun Bear, and Virginia Hine.

can be interpreted in terms of this directional grid, noting how the powers are appropriated, ignored, or obstructed by his psychic state or perceptual set.

Inherently, we grow, following the change of the seasons: the first innocent steps (south), "the fall" (west), cognition (north), and illumination (east)—and then we come back to the first innocent steps (south). But every time we come back to where we began, we have evolved another step, grown another inch, enlarged the circle of our life purpose. We do not return to the identical place we were before. Every rotation around the circle brings a step change in personal growth: *Non sum qualis eram* ("I am not what I was"). Our endless circling is actually a spiraling, a wheeling ever higher, even as our roots grow deeper. We return to find the path has taken a turn, the terrain has changed, the weather has shifted. We have learned how to walk. Now we must learn how to run.

The Powers of the South

Summer. Our journey through the six directions begins in summer, in long, hot days and brief nights. The great sun stirs green-blooded vegetation toward growth and fruition. Bird, animal, and insect wax and swarm. Roots hunger for the fervid earth as the "stone eaters" grope toward the heat of noon. All is ripening as the powers of the south swelter, simmer, and seethe.

Childhood. Childhood is the summer of life. Our growing awareness of the life journey before us supplants our memory of where we came from. Here we take the first steps toward maturity. Innocently we rejoice in the raw strength of blood and sensation. Yet unsevered, we rest in the security of parents, home, and family, too afraid to face the shadow monsters of adulthood on our own. Gradually we learn to use our wits, to control our emotions, to learn from our senses, to master the social roles of independent life. "The child is father of the man" (Wordsworth).

Innocence. A power of the south is the innocent, playful, trusting child in us all. We leap before we look because we are "not old enough to know better." Like Adam and Eve before the Fall, we wander delighted through the Garden, naming everything. We

133

twitter along the path of life, cheerful as little birds, unprepared for the dangers ahead. When troubles smack us in the face, we are outraged and surprised.

Trust. First we learn the reliability of things, before we learn their validity. Mother will come when we cry. Green light means go. All is controlled by a beneficent god who cares what happens to us. We call this trusting "childlike," yet much of it is necessary for our survival.

Play. In the south we are given the knack to turn away from real or imagined threat and to romp and play. With this comes the ability to see through pretense ("The Emperor's New Clothes"). Endlessly gaming, we begin to master ego, feelings, and mind, auditioning for roles and scenes in which we are the principal player, learning that Truth is more than what lies at the end of our noses.

Sensation. Sensibility, impression, sensuality, susceptibility, responsiveness are powers of the south. "Senses are the chief outlets of soul in this age" (Blake). Sight, hearing, smell, taste, and touch: They compose the music and rhythms to which we dance through our experiences.

Emotions. The child in us feels emotions, hurts deeply and readily. We instinctively express fear, hostility, affection, joy, despair, revenge, pity, sorrow, gusto, vehemence, fullness of heart, and all the other passions. Without our emotions we would never learn self-control, or grow into adulthood. Violence is a power of the south, as is war and other forms of aggression born of human emotion.

The Ego. In both Greek and Latin *ego* is the pronoun "I." The ego is one of the powers of the south. "I have," says the child in us who, without his "possessions," would be incapable of individuation or maturation. The child learns to keep and defend what is his. This distinction between "mine" and "yours" is the source of much growing pain. The ego is the proverbial Fool who carries all he needs on his back. But he does not know what is in his pack. He looks everywhere for what he already has.

Erotic Love. One of the greatest forces of the south, this power includes the attributes of sexual or romantic love: affection, attachment, passion, fervor, adoration, rapture, infatuation, gallantry, lust, adultery, jealousy, and all the faces of the love act itself. Cupid, the *puer aeternus* of love. "For love is blind all day and may not see" (Chaucer). Befuddled by the sweet sensations of love, led by the vagaries of sensation and fantasy, we are fascinated, charmed, allured, captivated, tempted, tantalized, frustrated, thwarted, rejected, even goaded to violence. Love as combat: "All's fair in love and war."

The Color Red. Vital, ruddy, inflamed, flushed, glowing, blooming, sanguine, red is the power color of the south. It is the color of the blood, of the red flag that goads anger, of the fanned coal, the color of fever, of desire, of lust: our "red light district."

The Element Water. Here is the ocean, primordial life, the sea water in our blood, the universal solvent in which we "suffer a sea change": liquefaction, irrigation, saturation. The south is the power of rising waters, of the ancient liquid in our lower or "lizard brain." In the summer of our life the heat of the sun evaporates the surface of our deep waters, condensing into clouds of emotions and sensation that break up into thundershowers and squalls of expression. The snow melts high in our mountains of aspiration and comes crashing down the canyons of our doing. But not a drop is lost. It collects in our wells and underground reservoirs and is drawn through childhood's dynamos to generate energy. Hot and sweating on a summer's day, the child in us bends over the garden hose. Cold, clear water gushes into his mouth. At that moment we know the power of water of the south.

> Rolling down in big and distinct drops,
> in drops like teeth,
> in heavy drops like marmalade and blood,
> rolling down in big drops, the water
> is falling,
> like a sword made of drops,
> like a river of glass that tears things,
> it is falling, biting,

beating on the axle of symmetry, knocking on the senses
of the soul,
breaking abandoned things, soaking the darkness.

—Pablo Neruda, *"Agua Sexual"*

The Force of Gravity. We do not look before we leap because we
are learning how to navigate space and time. Whatever goes up
must come down. The graviton pulls us back to our limits. Gradually, we learn to what extent we are ballast on the lifeboat of Earth.
The soaring spirit of childhood must dance with magnetism and
inertia. We master the intricate act of standing erect.

Medicine Animal—The Mouse. The symbol of the childhood in us,
the mouse is timid, acquisitive, never venturing far from the safety
of his nest. Busily gathering and storing seeds of experience for
times of darkness and drought, we scarcely see beyond the end of
our whiskers. We do not think a great deal about tomorrow, or
about our predators, which are legion. But each day we venture a
little farther from our nests. It was on such an excursion that Mouse
first heard the roaring of the Sacred River.

Medicine Symbol—The Drum. The skin stretched over the chamber
is the flesh covering the beating heart. The hand that beats the
drumhead is the hand of the Great Spirit on the hearts of his people.
When the drum throbs, symbols and ceremonial roles become
more real than life itself:

> I throw myself to the left,
> I turn myself to the right,
> I act the fish,
> Which darts in the water, which darts
> Which twists about, which leaps—
> All lives, all dances, and all is loud.
>
> —Gabon Pigmy

God the Son (Goddess the Daughter). Deity in its human aspect, the
south is Jesus as a boy, as the "Son of God" or "Son of Man," Kore
or Persephone as a girl, as daughter of the goddess or daughter of

136

woman. South is the mortality of god or goddess, the sheer physicality of the mystery of incarnation.

Under the influence of the power of the south, we build our homes over a dormant volcano, naively unaware of what boils beneath. Seemingly invisible forces move us to emotions, sensations, and actions. Innocently, we eat, sleep, play, walk, talk, and eventually learn to copulate. In the south, we ripen like wild apples in the sun. The sap rises in our bodies and courses through our limbs. We prepare to face the initiation of fall and severance from the arms of the mother tree.

This is the secret of the power of the south: It is always summer and we are always children.

The Powers of the West

Fall. Warmth and sunlight decline as we reap the fruits of summer. Chill wind, frost, and falling leaves remind us of the coming death of winter. There is a sharpness in the fall air. We have awakened from our exuberant summer lessons of "Enough! or Too Much!" (William Blake). We confront the reality of aging, decomposition, and death. The leaf must turn and wither; the fruit must tax the limb and finally drop. As the sun descends its southern ladder, darkness rushes in from the west. Even at noontime there are shadows. Now we will experience the other side of light, while "gathering swallows twitter in the skies" (Keats).

Adulthood. Innocence is initiated by experience. The virgin is deflowered. Childhood emotion and sensation become the "feeling" and insight of adulthood. With "The Fall" comes awareness of evil—and maturity. With maturity comes the capacity to introspect, to be self-conscious, to accept change, to dance with the consequences of our deeds, to engage the dragons of the life quest, to grow inwardly. Now the challenge is to find our places on the earth by finding our places in our bodies. The power of the west is the feeling power of adulthood, the inward strength of the "looks-within-place." Guilt, self-judgment, repression, addiction, and other "psychological knots" dwell here, for the psyche is an attribute of the west.

Introspection and Insight. Looking within, we see self reflected in the dark mirror of private nature. Seeing ourselves as others see us, we learn from what is seen through self-examination, in-question, in-spection, "feelings in the bones." The west is a stomach, a digestion place. Experience sought or unsought, assimilated or undigested, commingles and ferments here, to send sickness or health to the physical, mental, and spiritual bodies.

Self-Consciousness. The awkwardness of the adolescent "outsider" evolves into the sophisticated self-awareness of the adult. Without self-consciousness there is no self-knowledge. Sometimes this self-consciousness turns inward on itself, into narcissism, paralysis, self-victimization, or autism. Addiction burns here, fueled by guilt and forbidden cravings.

Self-Love. Not love of one's own body (as in eros of the south) but love of one's own psyche, of one's own nature: self-image, self-acceptance, self-esteem; acceptance of dark, "sinful," or shadow places; acceptance of life transitions, of aging. This self-love that makes it possible for us to love others is also inward love for the Great Mother, authoress of the dark mirror of consciousness.

Change. The fall is a transition from full to empty. West is the power to be altered, to be modified, to be turned, to be modulated, to be deviated. "The absurd man is he who never changes" (Barthelemy). The mature psyche surrenders to the crises of change: mating, parenthood, aging, midlife, bereavement, accident, or natural catastrophe. West is the power of mutation, the necessary forces that alter mood, thought, sensation, inspiration.

The Color Black. The sun sets and blackness prevails over the earth. The *anima/animus* wraps the psyche in dark wings. The unconsciousness heaves its leviathan bulk and shudders against the eyes of blindness. Then we know the power of black as pitch, black as coal, black as smoke, black as the devil, black as sleep. "I saw how the night came, came striding . . ." (Wallace Stevens). The power of the west is the necessary darkness, without which there would be no illumination.

Dreams. In dream hieroglyphics inscribed on the black portals of the west, we read the story of our ancestors, our dark side, our shadow. With the key of dreaming we unlock doors behind which lurk the poisonous serpents we are afraid to look at in the daylight. Behind our dreaming eyes, whether they are wide awake or closed in sleep, the soothsayer's harp shivers under the fingers of our collective ancestors. The west symbolizes our dream quest through a dark forest of archetypes.

The Element Earth. West is the power of earth. In this element the mass of all things is symbolized. In this mass is found the mystery of Gaia, the great goddess who receives, absorbs, holds, and changes the water of the south into energy stored in the folds of her dark womb. If south is heart and blood, then west is stomach and feces, digestion and elimination. The great mass of Tellus Mater is never static. She vibrates with visible and invisible forces. From the incipient womb of our Mother we and all the species arise, exist, and fall back.

The Weak Force. The atomic force of the west, symbolized by the W and Z particles, or "radioactive force," breaks down or decays the nuclei of radioactive atoms. Such disintegration or decay is apparent everywhere. In our own bodies we see the power of the "weak force," in physical aging and bodily change. Youth is not eternal. Adulthood experiences this. We try to grow younger in spirit even as our bodies surrender to the force of decay.

Medicine Animal—The Rattlesnake. The power animal of the west is the nocturnal rattlesnake, hunting through the night for its prey. Acknowledging the rattlesnake within us, we exercise the ability to sense with an inner "feel," to seek out blindly sources of warmth, to hibernate with our kind through long winters, to be quiet, perfectly quiet, inwardly waiting in the stillness for the truth to move or make a sound. We camouflage ourselves, shed our skins, strike cleanly, and paralyze the thing we hunt. We devour (internalize) our prey whole. When the time comes, our snake womb opens from within and live young come forth.

Medicine Symbol—The Rattle. The hollow gourd is the womb of the earth, shaken to stir seeds into life. What happens inside, in the dark magic of the shaker? Does the rattlesnake's Mother live there, she who gives and takes life? The womb of seeds, quickened by the heartbeat of the drum, will outlast the winter, and the people will be fed.

God the Mother. "Everything is born from the Mother" (Northern Cheyenne). The power of the west is God as Mother, as the Mother of God, as God's immortal Wife, as God's feminine face: Isis, Ishtar, Demeter, the Madonna, Gaia, or most simply, Mother Earth.

One can appreciate the powers of the west by watching the sun go down, by continuing to watch the western sky as it turns from orange to dark blue, finally to black. The stars appear one by one. The constellations march to their places in the western precinct of the night. As the light fades, thoughts and emotions turn inward, become muted and somber. Darkness has come—and will always come. There will always be changes, endings, farewells, deaths, and dashed hopes. The light from the stars will always pierce us with an inner pang. Life is short, and we dream half of it away. So we give ourselves to the darkness, having faith that morning light will come.

The secret of the power of the west is this: It is always fall and we are always in our maturity.

The Powers of the North

Winter. We have traveled from the hot climes of the summer, through the inward darkness of the fall, to the dead of winter. "One must have the mind of winter" (Wallace Stevens), for without winter there is no spring. Life is sleeping, waiting, but times are hard. Game is scarce. There is so little to eat. We live off the fruits of the summer, stored in the dark bins of the fall. We must not succumb to the death-dealing cold. We must discipline ourselves and work together for the survival of the people. We must work or we will be worked upon by Old Man Winter.

Old Age (The Greater Years). The severe power of our winter years, living out our days in the cold, snowbound mountains of the northern passage. Yet we are content. "No wise man ever wished to be younger" (Jonathan Swift). We are passing through our elderhood. Our experience has equipped us with the survival wisdom of our sacred forebears. Our purpose is to give away (impart) what we possess, think, know, and understand. We take our places as senior partners, chiefs, presidents, grandparents, ambassadors. We become teachers who serve and servants who teach. We cannot hide our infirmities and the obvious signs of bodily deterioration. Yet we persist in living through the winter because we know how much there is to be done before we finally accept death's summons.

Reason (Thought). The south is emotional power, the west psychological, the north rational. The power of the north is the Maker's rage for order, as symbolized by the human mind. The mind as measurer, gatherer, engineer, hunter, orderer, unifier; fountain of acumen, discernment, understanding, wit, diplomacy, calculation, aplomb. The Greeks and Egyptians personified mind power as the owl-headed god Thoth. The alchemists called it "Sophic Mercury," or "the Mercury of all true philosophers." With this power we orient ourselves in space and time, build our circles of life purpose, and make language with which to address God.

Wisdom. The power of a mature mind is enriched and brims over with experiences from the retorts of memory. Our people are starving from lack of food and love, freezing from want of shelter and understanding. "Old age and the wear of time teach many things" (Sophocles). Wisdom unifies, synthesizes, and integrates emotion, feeling, and thought into appropriate action. We are sagacious, solid, profound, balanced, and dispassionate. In the counsels of our people we will stand for reason, order, and the survival of the people and the earth.

Work (The Giveaway). Employment, industry, exertion, doing, straining, diligence, seizing the opportunity, making progress: The colder the winter, the harder we work to stay alive. We work for ourselves, our families, and our world. We work for the common good. We work because we find in it perfection, accomplishment, and a kind of joy. In the end, our work kills us. "Work, while the night is dark'ning,/ When man's work is o'er" (old Protestant hymn). Our final job is to give our bodies away in a good death.

Communication. Hermes, messenger of the gods, whose name signifies "interpreter" or "mediator," epitomizes the force of the spoken word, the *logos spermaticos.* Hermes is the human nervous system, the bicameral brain, the inspirer of verbal fluency, the god of roads and trails. The power of the north is that within us which seeks to be understood, which wills sounds and inflections into being, so that they can be organized into bridges of language among ears, eyes, and bodies. "Nothing is secret that shall not be made manifest" *(New Testament).*

Character. Disposition, temperament, propensity, quality, attitude, values—the years take their toll on body, ego, and psyche. How many times do we die "little deaths"? How many times does the shadow of trial cross our path? With blows from the hammer of circumstance we are tempered by life. Personality characteristics become marked. We mature into what life has made us.

Love for Others. Eros (south) and self-love (west) are essentially self-oriented. The love power of the north is other-directed, marked by fellowship, community, rapport, benevolence, generosity, charity, altruism, responsibility, and mercy. We rejoice in the good fortune of those we love. Family is a power of the north, our first and greatest teacher about loving one's neighbor as oneself.

The Color White. "The color of all colors" (Melville), the north is the glistening white snows on the slopes of the life mountain we are climbing; white, the color of a winding sheet, the color of the curtain of mystery that hangs over the Holy of Holies. The ever-burning light of reason throws rainbows against the screen, but what lies behind the curtain? The white light of reason alone cannot plumb the mystery.

The Element Air (Atmosphere). The ether that aerates our blood sends vitality to our brains. The invisible substance breathed by our living Mother Earth falls as rain, hail, and snow—the lifework of the lungs, the giveaway of breath, the exhalation of sounds in the form of language. Weather, climate, atmosphere, invisible and all-pervasive, is the mind of Grandmother Nature, surrounding us, thinking us. "Air should be cold and aggressive like the air of mountaintops" (Nietzsche).

The Strong Force. The hypothetical atomic particle called the "gluon" or "strong force" binds quarks together into protons and elements of the nucleus of atoms, assuring stability and order among the basic constituents of matter. This "nucleonic force" suggests the workings of Mind throughout the subatomic and macrocosmic universe.

Medicine Animal—The Bighorn. Like the vanished American buffalo, the bighorn sheep gave themselves away so that the people might live. Every part of him was used: meat for food, hide for clothes, bones and horns for tools, pipes, and ornaments. Climber of mountains, maker of trails, the bighorn is the self-disciplined master of waterless journeys. Like him we stand upon the heights of the winter mountains and look back at our tracks in the snow. So far we have come, giving away to the people. Soon, a blanket of white will cover all.

Medicine Symbol—The Fan. The power of the air is personified by the power of the wing that soars upon it. With the wing of a sacred bird the healer reaches into the afflicted part and removes the sickness or corruption. A local American Indian doctor, nearing his eighties, uses the fan in the sweatlodge. With an eagle's wing he scatters cool water and sweeps away disease. One might suppose the torrid lodge too debilitating to a man of his years, but he has been called to serve others. The power of the giveaway of the north is symbolized by the eagle fan in his hand.

God the Father. The northern deity is God as Father, the Father of God, the Goddess's immortal Husband: the masculine face of God,

Jehovah, Allah, Brahma, Mazda, Zeus, Osiris, Tezcatlipoca, Grandfather Sky. God as Reason, "Urizen" (Blake), guardian of commerce and industry, science and philosophy, law and organized religion, technology and engineering.

When we call upon the powers of the north we are the high priest standing at the entrance to the Holy of Holies. We are the Buddha, ferrying passengers across the Sacred River. We are Jehovah, shepherding his people through the wasteland. We are parents providing for our children, giving of ourselves so that they may live and grow. We call on our clearest mental powers in order to serve others, for the responsibility of parenthood or elderhood is ultimately the survival of the race of *Homo sapiens*. Eventually, the snow will melt from the mountains of the north. The earth will warm to the fires of spring; but for now, we work.

The secret of the power of the north is this: It is always winter and we are always in our greater years.

The Powers of the East

Spring. "A temper known to those who, after long/ And weary expectation, have been blest/ With sudden happiness beyond all hope" (Wordsworth). Rebirth wears the cerements of waiting. Who would think the "cold, familiar wind" would quicken these shoots of green fire? "For out of this dead body shall grow all the plants and herbs that adorn the earth with verdure, and from his seed spring all the animal species" (Mithras). The forces of spring are the forces of recoil, elasticity, transmutation, conversion, transformation, and resolution. The earth has brought forth "an infant form/ Where was a worm before. . . ./ A shriek runs through eternity" (William Blake).

Death/Birth. The great wheel of the seasons turns unceasingly. Who can halt it at the precise moment of death? Better to say there was a dying. But death? "O death, where is thy sting? O grave, where is thy victory? *(New Testament).* The great wheel spins on. In the east we are always coming forth, our eyes round with wonder. Was there ever a hard, cold winter? Even as we ceased breathing we were drawn into the radiance of newborn eyes. Our

144

wrinkles, our lameness, our infirmities, all melt in the furnace of birth's desire. Like winter and spring, death and birth touch. Where they touch there is transformation: "There is no death, only a change of worlds" (Chief Seattle).

Creativity. East is imagination, fancy, mythogenesis, the propensity to devise, contrive, invent, fabricate, concoct, improvise; to see "not with but through the eye" (Blake), apprehending not with but through the body. Vision, psychic "extuition," intuitive cognition, hallucination, divination, prescience, mysticism, clairvoyance are all eastern powers. These are not randomly bestowed but earned. Sunrise requires a previous night. Spring requires a previous winter. Illumination requires a previous state of blindness.

The Trickster. The contrary, the backward, the upside down, the unexpected, dwell in the east. "Without contraries there is no progression" (Blake). "See how the brook/ In that white wave runs counter to itself./ It is from that in water we were from/ Long, long before we were from any creature" (Robert Frost). Whatever form the trickster power takes—coyote, fox, raven, raccoon, lightning, earthquake, flood—it reminds us that at any moment we may turn completely around and make a new beginning: "It is from this in nature we are from. It is most us" (Frost).

The Suprarational. The east symbolizes creation, matter indifferent to form, incorporeality, immateriality, spirituality, the astral plane, animism. First, the physical world of sensation (south); next the inner world of the psyche (west); then the rational world of the mind (north); finally, the creative world of the imagination (east). The powers of the east are guardians of *samadhi*, enlightenment, and mystical ecstasy.

Love for the Great Spirit. The power of human love for deity or First Cause augments erotic love (south), self-love (west), and other love (north). This is love for the Giver of Life and Death, worship, reverence, devotion, awe, respect, and prayer: the mystical love of St. Theresa of Avila for her Christ, the love of Odysseus for Athene. Arrested by this power, human lives are transformed.

145

The Color Gold. The golden blood shed by the resurrected sun blooms in the flowers of spring: saffron, marigold, jonquil, dandelion, poppy, desertgold. This same spring-gold light glows in the Azoth, the Schamayim, the Philosopher's Stone, the "perfected work."

> Where the Youth pined away with desire,
> And the pale Virgin shrouded in snow
> Arise from their graves, and aspire
> Where my Sun-flower wishes to go.
> —William Blake, "The Sunflower"

The Element Fire. All is stimulated, kindled, aroused, awakened, stirred, quickened, burned in the ardent energy of fire. The fire in the chromosome is the fire in the star. As sperm seeks the egg, so fire seeks fuel. Likewise, words find ears in which to burn and light finds eyes to ignite. "Millionfueléd, nature's bonfire burns on" (G. M. Hopkins). From the general conflagration comes warmth and illumination.

The Force of Light. The photon is the "gauge particle" that imparts the "electromagnetic force" responsible for keeping electrons in orbit around the nucleus. Orbiting electrons behave in quantum fashion. Either they remain in fixed orbits or take quantum leaps into new orbits, emitting or absorbing energy. The ultimate unpredictability of quanta makes it virtually impossible to measure simultaneously the precise speed and position of a subatomic particle of light (the "uncertainty principle"). Yet the behavior of quanta is the fundamental basis of material transformation: the photon as electromagnetic trickster.

Medicine Animal—The Golden Eagle. Nimble-winged, soft as an arrow, we soar above the multitude on pinions of illumination. Feather-fingers outspread to catch the nuance of astral light, we swing, spiral, and dive in the changing currents of the solar river. In the spring, we mate for life and build our nests on the highest cliffs and prominences. Riding high "upon the rein of a wimpling wing" (Hopkins) in our ecstasy, we see far into the distance. Our prey, the little mouse, has ventured too far from his nest. But we too will pass away. Our feathers will be bound into healing fans and from our bones Sun Dance whistles crafted.

Medicine Symbol—The Pipe. White Buffalo Woman appeared at dawn carrying the sacred medicine bundle on her back. With her gift of the medicine pipe to the Plains Indians, she brought the sacred ceremonies that bound them together as nations. When the pipe is properly smoked, all the directions and powers are contracted into a single fire in the bowl or heart of the pipe. As the smoke is inhaled, the celebrant "takes in" the universe. The distinction between self and Self is erased. The fragrance of the sweet tobacco reaches the nostrils of the Great Spirit. The smoker is opened to illumination and mystical vision.

The Holy Spirit Goddess. The deity of the east is Anima Sola, the Queen of Angels, the High Priestess, Stella Maris, the Dove, the Muse, Calliope, Daughter of the Sacred Spring, White Buffalo Woman, the Graces, Persephone, "the little girl with golden hair who dances forever at the eastern rim of the world" (Hyemeyohsts Storm). At Pentecost she descended in tongues of fire upon the chosen ones and the vision of Christianity was born. To the artist, she is the spirit of inspiration and visionary illumination.

In the east, the blinding light of understanding floods the soul of winter. But in the light of dawn another threshold looms to the south. The flush of illumination will subside. Clouds of glory will dissipate. "Our birth is but a sleep and a forgetting" (Wordsworth). We will descend the mountain to the lands of childhood. Once again we will fall asleep in the bed of our mortal blood. But one does not enter the Holy of Holies of the east and return to the profane world unaffected. There has been a step-change. The self has taken a quantum leap to a new orbit. There will be a burst of energy, and growth will begin anew.

The secret of the power of the east is this: It is always spring and we are always being born into enlightenment.

The Poles

The fifth and sixth directions exist because *Homo sapiens* walks erect, thus creating upward and downward directions or poles.

Whatever direction the quester walks within the circle of his purpose, the polar directions remain constant. Traditionally, the poles are located at the center of the purpose circle, where the quester or lamenter stands and faces the other four directions he is invoking. He calls on the power of the fifth direction (earthward) by standing at the center and addressing the earth at his feet. He invokes the sixth direction (skyward) by calling into the vault of heaven above him.[3]

The Powers of Earthward

The earth represents the nether pole of our bodies, Tellus Mater, the primitive ground of our material being. It is that power in us that is coarse, unrefined, elemental, gross, rough, and mundane. In mythical terms, earthward is the direction of the underworld, Hades, Niflheim, organic or brute matter, ruled by the lords of mortality.

Christians call the powers of the earthward direction the "lower" or "sinful" nature, "the flesh," of which Satan reigns supreme. Others conceive these nether regions as populated by "elementals," such as gnomes, satyrs, pans, dryads, elves, brownies, or goblins. Freudian psychology might identify this brute power with the "id," with urges and behaviors derived from the dark, thanatropic regions of human nature. The astronomical concept of the "black hole" or inwardly collapsing pulsar, is the earthward taken to its extreme. The earthward power is what is left in the retort after the elemental exchange has taken place. Alchemy refers to this residue as "the toad."

But the powers of the earthward direction are not necessarily malevolent. The dark mass of "the toad" is infused with spirit magic. It stands beneath our feet and bonds us to the earthen of ourselves, to what is basic, fundamental, elementary, primary, primitive, original, undermost, bedrock, supported, upheld, and buttressed. It confirms in us that which is dense, solid, concrete, consolidated, and substantial—the clay and sod of us, the chalk and rottenstone, the plasma and germ, the topsoil and substrata, the adamantine quicksilver of bodily existence. For our roots do not end at the surface of the ground. They grope down into the darkly abysmal. "Under every deep a lower deep opens" (Emerson). Finally we arrive at the deepest level of the earth—the power of nothing:

> And I said . . . "Go down below, and make yourself firm and be a foundation for the lower things," and it happened, and it went down and fixed itself, and became the foundation for the lower things, and below the darkness there is nothing else.
> —*Book of Enoch* (Hebrew)

Even as the earthward force pulls us down to nothing, the skyward force draws us toward the light of everything. Mother Earth is nothing's egg. Father Sky is everything's sperm. From their interpenetration life is born—and dies. The egg cracks open and we come forth at the center of our purpose circles.

The secret of the earthward power is this: Earthward lies above us.

The Powers of Skyward

The sky represents the uplifted poles of our backbones. We stand erect, two-legged, head held high. Skyward is the crown, the pinnacle, the crest, the culmination, the zenith of our aspirations. With this empyrean power we ascend, rise, scale, mount, surmount, rear up, aspire on wings of soul. In mythical terms, skyward is Heavenward, toward Olympus, Mount Meru, or paradise—where the immortals live in rarified, subtle, and ethereal eternity.

Christians call the skyward powers the "highest," "divine," or "redeemed" nature, ruled by the Most High. Others consider the canopy of heaven as housing gods, goddesses, angels, sylphs, feys, and other aerial beings who ascend or descend the sky on chariots, stairways, or wings. Likewise, nature's water of life is sublimed from the ocean deeps and raised into the sun, where it condenses and returns to the deeps as rain and snow. Skyward is the power direction of resurrected and transfigured saints and saviors.

As a green shoot from the toad climbs the trellis of time, so the soul ascends the skyward pole toward the power of the ideal, the ethereal, the climax. We tug free from earthly bonds. "I will lift mine eyes unto the hills, from whence cometh my help. My help cometh from the Lord, which made heaven and earth" *(Old Testament).*

149

But the skyward powers are not necessarily benevolent. The welkin seethes with insubstantiality. We cannot see our footing when our eyes are continually fixed on a star. We must learn the dance of balance between earth and sky, between darkness and light, between our flooring and our flying. We must learn to mix earth with air, and water with fire. We will descend into the depths of our bowels and then we will climb the Mountain of the Thousand-Petaled Lotus. But we will return again to the depths of our bowels. In one hand we grasp the toad. In the other we hold a feather from the eagle of heaven.

Thus, the dark body of our earthwarding is made fertile by our yearning for the skyward spirit. Like the Altaic shaman, we climb the sky:

> above the white sky
> beyond the white clouds
> above the blue sky
> beyond the blue clouds
>
> this bird climbs the sky . . .
>
> blue hill where no hill
> was before: blue sky
> everywhere: a blue cloud
> turning swiftly
>
> that no one can reach:
> a blue sky that no one
> can reach. . . .
> —*Technicians of the Sacred*[4]

The secret of the skyward power is this: Skyward stands below us.

Conclusion

These are the six directions. At their center stands the initiate. Each direction pierces him with invisible lines of force. He is suspended in their webbing like a larva in a cocoon. Swaddled by the powers, he is not at their mercy any more than he is in command of them. The more he becomes aware of their presence in his experience, the more he will respect and dance in harmony with them.

Night has fallen now. The initiate sits inside a darkened circle of stones. The dark wind blows. He shivers in the cold. He feels so insignificant, so powerless. Where in this trackless universe does his trail lead? He cries out to the powers of the south: "Arouse the child in me with innocence and trust." He turns and prays to the west: "Help me go inside and see myself, for I must change." He turns and prays to the north: "Give me strength and understanding for those I love and serve." He turns to the east and prays: "Grant me the power of illumination; resurrect me." He looks earthward and cries: "Feed my roots. Hold me in your swallowing depths." He looks skyward and prays: "Raise me from the dust. Take me beyond the stars."

The powers of the six directions will answer his prayers. Even as his body sags with emptiness and fatigue, they will fill him with a symphonic equipoise. Even as the wind blows dark and cold, they will show him his place beside the roaring Sacred River.

7

Incorporation: Taking On the Body

"Go. Go then," Frog said. "Return to your People. It is Easy to Find them. Keep the Sound of the Medicine River to the Back of your Head. Go Opposite to the Sound and you will Find your Brother Mice."

Jumping Mouse Returned to the World of the Mice. But he Found Disappointment. No One would Listen to him. And because he was Wet, and had no Way of explaining it because there had been no Rain, many of the other Mice were Afraid of him. They believed he had been Spat from the Mouth of Another Animal that had Tried to Eat him. And they all Knew that if he had not been Food for the One who Wanted him, then he must also be Poison for them.

Jumping Mouse Lived again among his People, but he could not Forget his Vision of the Sacred Mountains.

—Storm, *Seven Arrows*

How could the minuscule hero of Storm's fable have known ahead of time what kind of reception he would get when he returned to his people? He didn't reckon on the fact that the mice in Mouseland had been going about their lives without a thought for him. They saw only what their narrow perceptions allowed them: a wet, bedraggled mouse telling impossible stories about talking frogs, high jumps, and swims in Sacred Rivers. No one listened or cared. Some were even afraid. How could Jumping Mouse be wet if it hadn't rained? No mouse in his right mind would jump into—what did he call it—a "river"? They reasoned that Jumping Mouse had been swallowed by a monster. Their fear had conditioned them to reject notions foreign to their nose-to-the-ground existence.

This same lack of comprehension will greet every initiate returning from a wilderness rite. If this impediment to the modern hero's progress didn't exist, there would be no challenge to the return. All

155

of his friends would run back with him to the Sacred River. They would all fast for a vision and everything would be hunky-dory. But that is not the way the real life story goes. The incomprehension of his friends *has* to be there, like a great, insurmountable wall. If it were not there, Mouse would hardly need to be heroic. The time has come to *live* his medicine, "to submit to his own myth," as the poet put it.

The perilous journeys of Odysseus were only a way of acquiring the "medicine" the hero needed to face the realities of home. "We discover not only that there is no welcoming committee on the dock to meet us but that we are going to have to fight our way into our own rightful place."[1] Will our modern hero fall into the same trap as Orpheus, who successfully endured the rigors of his underworld journey only to sacrifice all he had quested for in one tragic moment of doubt? He must begin his quest in the gross, everyday, routine, uncomprehending world of his new life station. Clearly, this is his first step toward the Sacred Mountains shining in the distance. He must obey the human voice of his nature, go down to the great river called Civilization, and jump in.

He has good reason to be afraid to return to Mouseland. It is a fearsome, dangerous, wild place, more savage and defeating than the wilderness of Mother Nature. In Mouseland he must work, surviving the routines, pressures, crises, relationships, and trials of his new life station. He must nurture the flame of his purpose and carry its warmth to the darkest corners. He must come to see that Mouseland is also a sacred world.

Incorporation: The First Hours

Rebirth into the secular body of civilization is almost always marked by complications of one sort or another. In a real sense, the initiate is an innocent child who must begin the painful process of growing up. Confusion and bewilderment can be mitigated by personal preparedness and ceremonial attention to the reentry process. If certain precautions are taken, difficulties are eased. The following events are critical to the first hours of his reentry into the sea of indifference that is Mouseland.

Emergence into the Social Body

When the quester "reappears" in the eyesight of others, he must be led through a postpartum process similar to that of a newborn infant. First, he is coaxed through the opening (see "Cutting the Last Cord," chapter 2) with a simple welcoming ceremony involving a dedication to his new life and warm embraces. Then he is given time and space to collect himself. He is not immediately bombarded with questions or comments. He is allowed to come in slowly, trusting the natural flow of social events to draw him gradually into the circle of fellowship.

Then the "child" is given to the mother for "bonding." In this case, the bonding medium is food—eating the Great Mother's body and sharing it in communion with others. It is also important that he give away any gifts he has brought back with him, such as a special stone, a shard of wood, a poem, a song, or some handmade thing. This reestablishes contact with others, strengthens social ties. The giving symbolizes his desire to share his vision and presages the "giveaway" of the reminder of his life. If he has received power for his people, it is appropriate at this time to channel it to others.

The newborn must be examined for vital signs of general physical and psychic well-being. A midwife is alert to candidates who are still at loose ends, off in the clouds, morose and withdrawn, or hysterically high-spirited. Some will have bellyaches, headaches, constipation, nausea, extreme bodily weakness, or other distressing but transitory symptoms. Those who experience difficulty orienting themselves to the social sphere require special attention.

Though it can be exhausting work, space must be cleared for everyone to unburden themselves of matters closest to their hearts. Emotional expression is to be encouraged, lest the returnee become poisoned or victimized by withheld feelings. The object is to "ground" him, to make sure he has accepted the givens of his new life status. This is not the time to listen to detailed accounts of his threshold adventures. In time, he will sort out the relevant from the irrelevant. Right now he needs to address himself to burning issues that might stand in the way of his assumption of a social body.

The newborn is separated from the Mother. The umbilical cord to the wilderness is severed when Raccoon and Mouse turn their backs on the Sacred River and deliberately walk away. Staying longer only delays the inevitable, indulging dangerous nostalgia in one who has just come through the womb. Real dangers lie ahead. There is real work to do.

The ritual ground must be cleansed of human signs. At basecamp no mark should remain that will outlive the next rain. This cleansing of the severance place can be accomplished with a simple ceremony that thanks the spirits of the place for their mercy. Everyone is given one last chance to go off alone and say farewell to the Sacred River. Then packs are shouldered and everyone turns away from the place of illumination and testing.

Within a day and night's time, the newborn must be bathed and wrapped in the swaddling clothes of civilization. Some kind of ceremonial ablution is in order, and after that, entry into the realm of civilized comforts and conveniences. Ritual bathing takes many forms: a river, a hot spring, a sponge bath, a shampoo, a steam bath, a sauna, or a sweatlodge. We are partial to saunas and sweatlodges. In effect, the initiates go into the earth one last time, into the dark Mother's womb, where they celebrate their gratitude for safekeeping, purge themselves of the dust of the wilderness passage, and pray for the welfare of their people. A strong sweat erases nostalgia, especially if the sweat is hot. Those with real physical disabilities or phobias should not be required to participate, but instead can wash themselves clean in other ways.

We strongly suggest that midwives not attempt to conduct a sweatlodge or sauna ceremony unless they are well versed in its ways and use. The meaning of the experience must be explained beforehand to all members of the group. Indebtedness to the American Indian must be acknowledged if the model used bears any resemblance to theirs. If the sweat doesn't include Indians, their sacred songs and spirit names must not be invoked. Let those who are not Indian sing from their own hearts and from their own heritage, invoking the names of their own gods and goddesses.

After the ablutions comes the feast, a celebration of plenitude, and, by extension, the civilization that makes it possible to burden the table with food from distant lands and peoples. This feast represents the warm blankets, the soft bed, the electrically heated room, the generous nipple of Mother America. In this way the newborn is given to the material influences and supports of civilization.

The road home is lined with familiar symbols. Dine here, drink there, stop and shop, amuse yourself, fill up. The plenitude of our culture provides returning questers with opportunities to test their balance. How easy it is to overload (because everything is offered). The returnee accepts the smorgasbord, does not scorn its existence, is not seduced by it, and does not fall into deep remorse if he makes a mistake. He makes a distinction between want and need. He can do this with a finer sense of discrimination now that he has endured the solitude and fasting of the threshold.

Any transaction made in a market, restaurant, or drugstore during the first few hours of incorporation is a further opportunity to take root in the here and now. Returnees should be encouraged to see the humanity and beauty of each person they encounter. As detestable or absurd as civilization may appear, their loved ones, friends, and family live in it, and their own places of power await them at home.

Crossing the Threshold of Home

At least twenty-four hours should be given to reflection and integration before taking up the new life. If the returnee does not live alone, this time may have to include others. Still, he must find solitude. Powerful illuminations often come during the first hours at home. These must be assimilated. Ideally, the time of semiseclusion should involve up to a week of "digestive living" before he is ready to assume the responsibilities and privileges of his new life station. Although the first days of his return may be filled with vivid illuminations and feelings of self-worth, he may find it difficult to sleep, feel claustrophobic or restless, and have difficulty establishing a routine. Some say their feet hardly touch the floor, that they dream-walk. Such symptoms indicate that the person is not ready to encounter the world at large fully; he must wait for the acuteness of the threshold experience to fade.

Those who have waited at home for the initiate to return are like the mice who greeted the mysteriously wet and bedraggled Jumping Mouse. Their incredulousness, indifference, or threatened silence may tax the very love our hero brings back to give them. He must realize that while he was away they were living a life that hardly gave them time to miss him. They may consider his stories to be irrelevant to the important events of their own lives. Spouses or mates often feel personally threatened, fearing that undesirable changes in their "other half" have taken place while he was gone. Sometimes their envy overshadows their enthusiasm or empathy. Sometimes unfinished business has smoldered in the breast of the one who stayed behind, breaking out when the other returns. Into the very wilderness of his home the quester quests. There, in the closets, cupboards, and corners, lurk the monsters of his karma—to be flushed out by the light of vision.

False expectations are another big obstacle. Loved ones and friends may exhibit a distressing tendency to expect that certain changes have occurred in the returnee. This reaction is typical of the return of young people. Parents, teachers, counselors, probation officers, and others often anticipate that the young person will no longer behave in ways that formerly distressed them. Of course, he will not be able to please everybody (or himself) all the time. He must be prepared to face these expectations without blaming himself.

Incorporating persons should be especially wary of blabbing all the precious details of their wilderness passage to unsympathetic or cynical ears. Far better to protect the visionary essence within, where it lies in the warm nursery of the heart. Revealing too much drains vital energies, tarnishes the sacredness of the vision, and dries up healthy juices of rejuvenated ego. Let them savor their newfound knowledge, without nostalgia or the need for the approval of others.

Occasionally, people have returned to tragedy or catastrophe. One young man returned only to be killed in a traffic accident three days later. Another returned to face a trial that sentenced him to two years in the county jail. One woman came back to the news that her father had died, another to a burglarized home. Indeed, the conditions of life may deal out a supreme test at any time. Those who had faced their worst fears reported that special care taken during the first few hours of incorporation helped them to confront and accept the unexpected disaster.

Council of Elders

In traditional passage rites, the initiated one was often brought back to a group of community elders who heard his story, discussed its meaning, and validated (formally accepted) his new life status in the community, sometimes conferring a new name.[2]

In modern culture, weak forms of this postthreshold ceremony persist in the "postsalvation" incorporation of new believers into evangelical churches, or in the receptions following the Jewish bar and bat mitzvah. There is, however, no universally sanctioned body or council of elders with the power to validate such experiences fully or confer recognition of changes in life status. A modern individual passing through a life change must validate himself or join a body of "believers," a subculture, or a peer group that will recognize and validate his status change.

For purposes of validation, a kind of elders' council can be convened. The "elders" would be a circle of witnesses whose task is to recognize, approve, and empower the mythical life quest of the hero. They ask questions, make comments, share insights, and generally support aspects of the candidate's story that are positive and beneficial to himself and others. A good basis for discussion is the old tried and true formula: The story of the threshold is the story of the quester's life. The objective is not to solve his problems, but to emphasize his ability to solve them himself. Questions cover the physical/practical, emotional/psychological, and spiritual/mythical dimensions of the hero's participation in all three phases of the quest, and differ according to threshold allegory and model.

In the elder's circle the threshold story always bears the features of the monomyth, however roughly:

> *The hero left everything behind.* What did he leave behind? Who did he let go of? (How about his personal life?) Why did he leave it behind? What did he want to change? What was it like to sever? What severance-like ceremonies did he perform? With what result? Was he prepared to face the threshold? What inner resources or defenses did he count on?
>
> *He went alone to the Sacred River.* What did he do when he crossed the threshold? How did he feel? What did he think? To whom did he pray? What did he expect? What did he receive? Was he ready for what the experience turned out to be?

He endured the threshing-hold. How does his physical experience of the threshold mirror his psychological, rational, and spiritual perspectives? How were his loneliness, fear, emptiness, and boredom mirrored by the physical landscape? What were his monsters, shadows, adversaries, obstacles? What was his way of bearing the trial?

He was granted a gift, an insight, a vision, a guide. Who (living or dead) came to him? What was communicated? How were his prayers answered? What spirits, allies, angels, guides, animals, medicine signs, altered states, dreams appeared? What emotions, feelings, ideas, revelations, insights, strengths, wisdom? What ceremonies did he perform?

He saw what he had to give to his people. What specifically and practically does he bring back for the service of his people? What is the essence of his vision? What came to him at his most illumined moments? What was the light, the gleam, the clue, the thread, the faith? What is it that he will do?

He returned to his people and a new life station and took on the body of his purpose. Has incorporation been easy or hard? What are the obstacles, fears, realities? Can he describe his task of "performing the vision on earth for the people to see?" In what ways does he use the power of his threshold quest? Who are his people? What are their needs? How does he meet these needs? What is the source of help he needs to do what he must do?

The supportive role played by the "elders" consists of seeing the basic outlines of the initiate's life story, of reflecting that story back to him, and of helping him to understand its beauty, humanity, and uniqueness.

The elders' ceremony has a particularly worthwhile effect on young people celebrating their passage into adulthood. Parental attendance at the ceremony only further enhances the meaning and long-term value of the youngster's participation.[3]

Incorporation Midwifery

The incorporation process demands a midwife's utmost skill and attention. He stands in attendance at the "coming out," realizing, with a kind of awe, what his charges have just been through. Spontaneous admiration and respect for their stout hearts well up in him. "Welcome!" he calls out. "Welcome to your new life!"

In the first critical hours of the incorporation phase, there is a kind of euphoria (high spirits, boisterous behavior, optimistic resolve), that can mask more profound emotions and feelings of apprehension, unreality, extreme shyness, or irritation. It is not exactly easy for certain individuals, particularly introverts, to warm up immediately to a loud social scene. Others may be returning with feelings of personal failure (despite their obvious accomplishment), considering themselves unworthy of their new life station. Still others may be dancing with an anger and belligerence that they never knew existed in themselves, having so far led meek and self-effacing lives. Still others may return fearing that while they were alone and fasting they went insane.

It is best not to impose oneself too aggressively on any returnee. Better to touch him lightly, allowing for emotions to be expressed without pressure to explain why. The midwife keeps his eyes open, watching for signs of imbalance, flightiness, withdrawal, self-exaggeration, or other indications that the returnee may be having difficulty taking on his body as a social entity. If the incorporation activities of the first few hours do not bring him back to the ground, then the cause of his discomfort must be ascertained.

The elder concentrates on an ungrounded person's bodily and emotional states, on his sensations and feelings. Esoteric questions or brilliant mind-play will do nothing to help secure the returnee. The solitude and the fasting have evoked a kind of altered consciousness. Yet he may not even be aware that his perceptions have shifted and that he is looking at the world of basecamp through his threshold eyes. Ordinarily, the "high" of returning is pleasant, clear, expansive, open, dreamlike, and positive. Sometimes there are unpleasant (though mild) visual distortions, feelings of alienation, vulnerability, indigestion (filling up too quickly), malaise (feeling rubbed raw, wired, and overloaded, unable to sleep). If the initiate is still at loose ends, he will have a preponderance of negative sensations, too apprehensive of, or too eager to embrace the social order and its civilized, artificial accoutrements.

An ungrounded candidate has not gone bananas. Considering the kind of world he is returning to, he's saner than those crazies who unthinkingly accept it. He needs a chance to vent his feelings, to let go of anger, fear, disgust, or uncertainty, to talk about the prospects of his new life station—going home, the people at home, the events and scenes he must face in order to be worthy of his new life station. He may need to accept himself before he can feel accepted and included. Almost always, he can be led to see the positive side. After all, he is very close to this positive power, having just been there.

There will always be a few who somehow never make it back into their bodies because, perhaps, they were never in their bodies to begin with. In certain hardened cases, the threshold ordeal will only accentuate the difficulties. They return only to blame others and to feel even more victimized. At such times we realize that ancient passage rites have never been a cure, but a means for society to measure personal growth. The rite's transformational power is directly proportional to the individual undertaking it. We do not blame ourselves or lose too much sleep over the few mice who try to jump but instead dig themselves deeper into their hole. All we can do is reflect their way back to them so they see it, though most of the time they will not see themselves clearly. They will see what they want to see. We have to let them go, knowing they may never find an adequate survival myth, that they may continue to add their weight to the great numbers of those who are unable to find their way through the transitions and crises of their lives.

Most who return will present a coherent story of personal growth, insight, and the acceptance of self and change. The midwife listens to their stories for indications that they are ready to take on the third phase of the rite. It will lift his heart to see that their myth is adequate, and that there is no life question they cannot answer for themselves.

"Was it all a dream?" she wonders. "Maybe it didn't really happen."

We answer, "Was it a dream? Did it really happen?"

"If it was a dream, then what does the dream mean?"

We turn it back to her. "What do *you* think it means?"

"But there are so many ways of looking at it."

"OK then, what's the main theme of your threshold dream?"

"It's about a woman who discovered she was really happy living on the land. She felt she belonged there, that she had finally found her place."

"What brought her to that conclusion?"

"Lots of things. A lizard crawled up on my boot and said, 'Welcome, sister!' A kingbird sat in the bush next to me every morning and sang a song over and over again: 'Bless you! Bless you! Bless you!' The sun caressed me with hot hands and burned my skin. The earth cradled my body and gave me scratches and bruises, but they were like kisses. The wind blew through me and cleaned out all the poisons. I took off my clothes and walked around like a daughter of the Goddess. I found out I wasn't afraid of the dark. At night the moon and stars sang to me. Wherever I went, I felt at home."

"Good. Did you encounter any monsters out there?"

"Ha! You mean besides my ex-husband? Yes, I thought a lot about my youngest son, who is still in juvenile hall. I thought a lot about all the people I'd hurt in one way or another. I felt very sad about what human beings are doing to the earth. I wandered around for two days feeling so lonely and godforsaken and inadequate I wished I could die. I don't want to grow old without love." She begins to cry.

"How did you deal with the monsters?"

She sighs, chokes back a sob. "I asked a lot of people to forgive me. I prayed to God to make it better. I saw what I had to do with my son. I realized I couldn't let the condition of the earth push me too far out of shape. It won't do me any good to get all tied up with hatred. It just makes me ineffectual. If I'm going to have to learn how to love, I might as well start with myself, and with my son, and maybe even my ex-husband."

"What did you see in the mirror of nature?"

"Well, a couple of things. I ran into this crazy gopher. Yes, a gopher. He was digging a hole, pushing the dirt out until he had a mountain of dirt. Every once in a while he'd peek his nose out and look around to see if everything was safe. Then he'd go back to digging. He was very persistent, a good worker. I couldn't believe I'd find a gopher out there in those desert mountains. The ground seemed so hard. What was there for him to eat?"

"What did the gopher say to you?"

"Well, it was just a feeling. But it seemed to me that he was saying I was like him. I'm very persistent about digging this hole. I mean, building my home, finding my place. Even where the ground is hard and there isn't much to eat."

"What else did you see?"

"For some reason my grandmother was very close to me. I

thought about her a great deal of the time. Once I was almost sure she was sitting behind me. I turned around but it was only a boulder."

"What's so important about your grandmother?"

"My grandmother on my mother's side. She went through a lot of hard times when she migrated to California from western Kansas. Their farm dried up and they had to move, six kids and all, to a place near Fresno. She was a strong woman, a strong and loving mother, patient and persistent. All six of her kids went to college. She was always my special grandparent."

"What did she say to you?"

"Nothing. She was just there. I think when she was there I remembered my childhood, when I was a little girl growing up in Sacramento."

"Do you think she might become a kind of spirit guide or inner counselor to you when times get bad?"

She smiles a smile that is probably much like her grandmother's. "I guess you could say I fasted for her. I earned her."

"Where did you find your magic?"

"Magic? Well, I did a ceremony. I made a little fire and burned that part of the past I was leaving behind. Then I captured the ashes and spread them all around and in my purpose circle. I gave it back to the earth. I know I can't just burn up my past. It has made me who I am. I just wanted to signify that I no longer needed it. As I burned each item I wanted to forget, I asked for forgiveness. And I said, 'Now it's time to go on and leave you behind.' It felt as though a huge burden had been lifted. Yes, that was magic. There was a lot of other magic, too."

"What gifts do you bring back to your people?"

She thinks about this for a while, sifting answers. "To me that means the decision to quit my job at the insurance company. I'm sick of it. I do absolutely nothing to satisfy my need to do something significant in my middle age. For a long time I've been interested in hospice work. I think when I get back I'll look into their training program. But I also have a few matters to work out with my children, especially the youngest."

"What else did you bring out of your dream?"

"Dream? Who said it was a dream? My ass is still sore from sitting up all night in my purpose circle! The hours passed like eons. I never thought morning would come. No, I actually did it. The whole thing was real. The feeling of oneness with the earth was real. The gopher was real. My grandmother was real. My growling belly was real. My loneliness was real. I really did it. I came through on my own!"

And so the "incorporation session" goes. This is but the sketchiest of samples. Needless to say, the usual tone of such exchanges is positive, optimistic, and beneficial to all who attend. Note the plenitude of ammunition for the forces of self-esteem. This is the kind of heroine who persists through hard times and sees beauty in the world around her. She is brave and lonely and ready to change her life, to encounter the risk of a new life station. This is not to deny the fact that she is human, that she suffers from guilt, anger, and regret, but the basic theme of her trial shines through the shadow lands. She will make it through the Slough of Despond and the Forests of Guilt. Her grandmother will accompany her as a companion and guide. She will find her place on the earth. She will find a way to serve her people. Her life will not be a saga of misfortune and defeat.

What About Failure?

Not everyone makes it through the passage. There are always those who, for one reason or another, choose to terminate their ordeal. Invariably, their reasons for returning are valid and sufficient, at least to them. One man returns because he has had a raging headache for two days and has finally convinced himself that it's not psychosomatic. A woman opts out, but not, she says, because it was too hard. She had simply completed the task she had set out to do and had no further reason to stay in the threshold. Another woman ends her fast because she has a urinary tract infection. A man comes out because he can no longer live with himself, knowing that his father is dying and he has not told him how much he loves him. Another man comes out because the passage rite he thought he had committed himself to turned out to be all wrong for him. A young woman returns because she had been dropping amphetamines and got terribly sick and wired. A young man returns because, as he says, "a huge scorpion jumped out from under a rock at me and I slipped and fell down a cliff" (almost killing himself). An older woman returns because she has a huge blister on her toe she thinks might be infected.

Whatever reservations we might have about an initiate's stated reasons for returning, we must not call it failure. There is no failure when a human being measures himself in the mirror of nature. There is an ultimate "failure," yes—when we finally go back to the Great Mother who gave us birth. But perhaps it is a success. Until then, every little setback is but a step in preparation. And who are we to judge such setbacks as failure? We are not the one who returned. We can never quite understand what led to the decision to terminate the initiation. As the old Indian man who teaches us says, "It is not up to you to decide who is a success and who is a failure. That is up to Mother Earth and the Great Creator."

Invariably, the one who returns early is unhappy with himself, even when his reasons seem completely legitimate. There is nothing a midwife can do about this right away. It's good for them to sit alone in the deepest misery if that is what they seem to prefer. Eventually they will seek his counsel. Most will honestly tell him they feel half-born, aborted, confused, deeply disappointed, and angry with themselves. Others may act smug and self-aggrandizing, hiding profound fears that maybe they too easily let themselves off the hook. Still others may return full of blame for everything and everyone but themselves, playing the victim with righteous indignation. Regardless of how they mask their disappointment, he will do his job. And his job is to find the good medicine story in their adventure or mishap and to reflect it back to them, so that they can learn, grow, and prepare themselves for the rite a second time.

Implementing the Vision

Usually, the candidate returns with eyes aglow. He has been to the Sacred River and has seen what he has seen. His being quivers with the revelations of dawn. He may fill a Raccoon's ears with incredible tales: "An eagle landed in my purpose circle." "I saw blue lights and felt mystical presences." "A coyote came up and talked to me." "I had a great vision of the world at peace." "I dreamed of rainbow horses dancing in a circle around me." Then there are those few who return crestfallen, alleging to have been ignored by divine favor: "Nothing happened." "God didn't speak to me." "I didn't have any significant encounters with animals." "I fell asleep in my purpose circle and missed the revelation." "I didn't get a medicine name." "I still don't know what I'm going to do with my life."

Many experience—or claim not to experience—"vision." There are few who do anything but talk about it. Words, words. What power have they, apart from the actual *practice* of the vision? There are plenty of talkers, but few doers. And what about those who claim to suffer from lack of vision, yet who are daily involved in visionary work? Clearly, vision is not just something one talks about. Vision is not just something one claims to have or not to have.

Rather than defining "vision" narrowly, one might instead associate "vision" with action or implementation, signs of the vision's impact on the minds and hearts of others. "Without vision the people will perish!" warned the Old Testament prophet. The vision he referred to had little to do with trippy medicine objects or phantasms of fancy, nor was he describing the mystical illuminations of the hermit who has left the world behind. The prophet was speaking of the kind of vision that empowers the muscles of the body and mind with the tension of will, day after day after day. He was not discussing interludes of suprasensational pyrotechnics. Vision is what never goes away, no matter how hard we try to run from it or forget. It is personal conviction in action. It is a sense of mission in the process of being accomplished. It is myth realized through work. It is practicing what we preach.

Keeping the Pot Boiling

There is no way for a midwife to avoid a considerable amount of contact with incorporation candidates for weeks after they return. This lingering contact may inconvenience him unless he can transfer their attention away from himself and toward various kinds of activities designed to strengthen their purpose and vision. The amount of required help varies according to the individual. A majority of those who return make the transition to their new job, marriage, home, or life station without undue difficulty. These balanced souls may drop in to say thanks, but rarely do they request therapeutic aid. A significant minority, for various reasons, want more. Their wilderness quest has aroused their hunger for further adventures in psychic growth.

There is a countless number of activities that will keep Mouse's pot boiling. But it is not Raccoon's business to solve problems. That would defeat the "therapeutic goals" of the wilderness quest. He can make referrals or suggestions, but he's a midwife, not a babysitter. If a crisis arises and the candidate needs to do something right away, he might tell him to take his problem on a "medicine walk" and then come and discuss it.

The best ongoing means of incorporation available is "self-help," as opposed to "other dependence." If the person is strong and ready, he will adequately incorporate himself. What is "adequate" nowadays, however, is but a pale shadow in comparison to ancient practices of sanction and validation.

The Purpose Circle

As an imagined or visualized construct, the purpose circle is an effective self-help tool. The memory of this dying place of the quester's threshold ordeal is encoded on the software of his body-psyche. The circle will accompany him wherever he goes and for as long as he desires. When he needs its grounding force, he can call it back, and once again he is alone and hungry in the dark silence, hanging between heaven and earth, balancing at the dead center of the directional powers.

Confused individuals can, with the aid of guided imagery, go back to their death circle and find the missing thread, experiencing again the balance and thrust of their purpose. They can ask questions or pray there, receiving answers in harmony with their deepest being. As a six-directional cocoon, the circle lends itself well to daily meditation. As time passes, much of the detail of the circle may fade, but a basic grid will always remain. Gradually, this grid will take on symbolic and mythical dimensions, the stones of the circle becoming rubies, diamonds, or points of astral light. The meaning of the circle may evolve into an immune system, a protective bubble, or a psychic envelope or aura. Years after they return from the threshold, many speak of using their purpose circles in this way.

Finding a Retreat

The vision will not survive without periodic cultivation in the garden of nature. A person must return again and again to com-

170

mune with and learn about the animals, spirits, or influences that comprise his sense of his "medicine." He will need a "power place" near his home where he can go alone for restorative healing and solitude. Distracted by seemingly ironclad schedules and daily gridlocks, he may forget he has this easy means of renewal. Busy people need to schedule their nature visits formally months ahead of time. Once these visits become an integral part of the calendar, they will be eagerly anticipated.

At his retreat, his power place, a person conducts himself as he sees fit. If he remembers that the place is a mirror of his perceptions, he will always learn something there. The self will meet Self, and find encouragement to go on.

> And I have felt
> A presence that disturbs me with the joy
> Of elevated thoughts; a sense sublime
> Of something far more deeply interfused,
> Whose dwelling is the light of setting suns,
> And the round ocean and the living air,
> And the blue sky, and in the mind of man. . . .
> —Wordsworth, "Tintern Abbey"

Finding a Teacher

Initiatory midwifery often involves helping people find good teaching on such subjects as rites of passage, initiatory experiences, shamanic techniques, primitive ritual and symbol, or American Indian practices. This is a natural reaction to the existential profundity of the quest. The initiate will gravitate toward those who claim to know the way beyond the river to the Sacred Mountains.

Any passage-rite graduate looking for a "medicine teacher" is caught in a contradiction. Didn't his threshold experience tell him it was he who had the medicine? On the other hand, the desire to study the subject more deeply is almost irresistible. If he cannot value his own ability to answer his own life questions, he may plunge into a guru quest of questionable value to him. There are two kinds of guru questers: those who seek a guru because they cannot live without one, and those who seek a guru because they want to become strong enough to do without one. The following remarks are directed at this latter group. The former types do not need to consider how to go about finding a good guru. They will find one as a moth finds the flame.

Good teachers must be selected carefully; like everyone else, they are subject to human failings. Some are less liable to manipulate or damage their students than others. Some are more genuinely what they claim to be. One might look around for hidden snags before he throws himself blindly into the water. A good apprentice does not holler "help" from the quicksand he thought was a swimming hole.

Beware of those who advertise themselves to the general public as genuine gurus, medicine men, sorcerers, holy men, and so on. Beware of traveling road shows and snake oil. Is it not possible that among those who claim to be bigwigs there are some who only *wish* they were? Is it not possible that those who really are what they claim to be are not busy making claims about their greatness? It only stands to reason that the *real teachers* are the ones who are *doing* it, who are performing their vision for the people to see. Invariably, these real ones are occupied with their service. Why should they want a bunch of "guru seekers" coming around and interfering with their work?

How swollen is the teacher's ego? Does he say, "My way is the only way," condemning other ways, particularly those which are similar to his? A common trait of self-styled "shamans" is intolerance for other shamans. Don't get caught in the warfare between them, or become a clone of the teacher, professing the same dislikes or prejudices. The real shaman actively walks the "rainbow path," allowing the white man into the sweatlodge, the black man into the synagogue, the red man into the tabernacle, the man of mixed blood into the temple of the pure-bloods. He does not make war against his colleagues. He reveres their path and seeks to align with them in causes promoting the mutual welfare of their people and the earth.

Be wary of teachers who self-righteously claim to be without failings. Although there are a few who have attained a blessed, transcendent state, they are easy to spot. On the other hand, there are plenty who strut around like peacocks although they are just barnyard fowl. Beware of pharisees who are "uptight" about how to perform ceremonies properly, how to pray properly, how to behave properly in church or sweatlodge. These folks have plenty of skeletons in their closets.

What makes a good medicine teacher effective is the fact that he is not hiding. He is who he says he is. He is not presenting himself as a model of perfection, or even as an expert. One of our dearest teachers says he is an "old fart Indian doctor." He asks that his name not be printed. "Medicine talk" he calls "bullshit." He figures he has done enough "crazy stuff" in his life to have earned the monicker of "old fart." He is very real and very true to his vision.

Balance is another key ingredient in a good medicine teacher. Does he live in harmony with the rational and the intuitive, the solitary and the social, the civilized and the natural, the masculine and the feminine, the sacred and the profane? Is his life and those around him enhanced by his connection to the powers of the six directions? Women might be careful about male teachers who are out of balance sexually. Men might be careful of female teachers for the same reason. Regardless of sex or sexual preference, a good teacher is professional, nurturing, and self-disciplined in such matters. He is deeply respectful of the teacher-student relationship and not apt to take advantage of it.

Apprenticeship entails going to the teacher and finding out what the terms are. The student may have to be persistent, yet respectful of the teacher's time and energy. If an apprenticeship is granted, the student must be perfectly clear about what will be expected from him. Then he must fulfill the terms of the agreement to the best of his ability, going out of his way to return in kind what is given him.

A good apprentice listens carefully and does what his teacher tells him to do. He is not afraid or too proud to ask questions or to appear dumb or thickheaded. He genuinely thinks about the lessons imparted to him. He does not attempt to mask who he is. Certainly, he does not suspend his own perceptions or intuitions, but for the time of his apprenticeship he is willing to follow the promptings of his teacher. The consciousness that stands aside and observes will tell the student when the term has ended. The teacher will also know.

Another sign of a good medicine teacher is his attitude toward letting his students go their own way. If he rejoices in the end of the apprenticeship and honors their ongoing life quest, he can't be half-bad. If he wants to bind the apprentice to him in continued servitude, then the student has every right to question the quality of the teacher's vision.

Material payment for medicine or shamanistic teachings takes many forms, depending on the bent of the teacher. Many traditional teachers accept money, among other kinds of gifts such as food, blankets, tobacco, or jewelry. Sometimes compensation does not take the form of money or gifts. The student may contribute work, or a skill of some sort. In the end, no teacher worth his salt will refuse a worthy student just because he cannot pay in full. But the student must never take advantage of this fact, making every attempt to compensate his mentor adequately.

Questing Again

It is as though some initiates have been bitten by the bug. They are sure there is more to learn if they go out again. They feel they can cross the threshold better prepared, with more reasonable expectations. Perhaps they will attain the prize they got a glimpse of the first time. Perhaps they feel called to midwifery itself, and want to train themselves with passage rite experiences.

Mythical literature is thick with accounts of saints and heroes who returned to the sacred threshold again and again, to regenerate or to attain the vision they sought. Black Elk speaks of the need for the young man to return to his power place and cry for *wakan:*

> This young man who has cried for a vision for the first time, may perhaps become *wakan.* . . . But he must cry for a vision a second time, and this time the bad spirits may tempt him; but if he is really a chosen one, he will stand firmly and will conquer all distracting thoughts and will become purified from all that is not good. Then he may receive some great vision that will bring strength to the nation. But should the young man still be in doubt after his second "lamenting," he may try a third and even a fourth time; and if he is always sincere, and truly humiliates himself before all things, he shall certainly be aided, for Wakan Tanka always helps those who cry to Him with a pure heart.[4]

Our own schedule includes one fasting rite each year in the mountains near our home. We no longer consider it an ordeal but a homecoming. Over the years, the back-and-forth movement between wilderness and civilization has stitched together the edges of the two fabrics into one whole cloth. The spirits and powers who first came to us in the wilderness now come to our family circle. Those graces and muses that blessed our home now minister to us in the wilderness. Gradually, we are mastering a two-worlds dance.

People wanting to quest again have asked about the advisability of going down to the Sacred River alone, fasting without supervision or basecamp support. We strongly discourage solo expeditions. The individual runs a much greater risk of not returning. There is no one to help if he breaks his leg or suffers a heart attack. And if no one knows exactly where he is, no one will come looking for him. Traditional rites of passage never included recklessness. Someone always went with the initiate, helped prepare and care for him, knew exactly where he was, and was ready to render aid if necessary. If a person decides to quest without professional supervision, it is absolutely essential that he includes another support person, a buddy, or another quester, in his expedition.

The Predictable Fall

Jumping Mouse Lived again among his People, but he could not Forget his Vision of the Sacred Mountains. The Memory Burned in his Mind and Heart. . . .

Now that Jumping Mouse has seen the Sacred Mountains, what is he going to do? It is almost as though he has been marked by God in some special way that sets him apart from the others. Maybe he should never have jumped in the first place. He sees how tough a directive Frog gave him when he said, "Go then, Return to your People. . . . Keep the Sound of the Medicine River to the Back of your Head." At first he was eager to see his brother mice again. Now he is not so sure he even wants to live with them.

The all-too-familiar omnipotence of the civilized world jars the returning pilgrim with doubts. Now he has to drive the car, punch the time clock, make the deadline, provide for the family, clean up the house, do the dirty dishes and the laundry, make the deposit and withdrawal, answer the phone, push the button, fill the tank, flush the toilet. No matter how profoundly his sense of himself might have changed, he still has to suck on the teat of Mother Civilization.

If he turns away in revulsion, he is lost. He must take his turn with the others. But having to do so requires a draining, a falling away from the vision, a predictable setback:

> The problem is to maintain this cosmic standpoint in the face of an immediate earthly pain or joy. The taste of the fruit of the temporal draws the concentration of the spirit away from the center of the eon to the peripheral crisis of the moment. The balance of perfection is lost, the spirit falters, and the hero falls.
> —Joseph Campbell, *The Hero With a Thousand Faces*

Inevitably, the time comes when our hero realizes he has just pressed the light switch without being aware there was a sunset. He kicks himself for being so forgetful, so unobservant, so preoccupied with people, problems, and events. He tries to remember the sunset of his threshold experience, but he can't remember details. He wonders if all the important lessons of his wilderness quest are draining away. As the weeks pass, his fears give way to certitude. He *is* forgetting a great deal—not just the detail but the exhilaration, the ecstasy, the energy, and the purpose. He gets depressed. Sometimes the depression gives way to despair. The words of one quester speaks for many:

> Why can't I remember the revelation? Why can't I feel the freedom? Why is it lost? Must we always and ever return to the valley of the shadows? Return? No! Fall! The word "return" implies some sort of conscious intent. In no way did I intend this loss of vision, this doubt, this descent. I *fell!* There must be some kind of spiritual gravity. Such energy it takes to struggle up toward a vision! Such careful, obedient, and innovative attempts at ceremony. Such self-examination. Such ordeals! Such effort it takes to break through into illuminating insights, new perceptions. And with what ease we fall after the quest is over and the vision won. Why? Why?

The predictable fall is necessary. The vision must be tested by adversity equally as powerful as the forces that brought it into being. The story is told that Mohammad returned from Mount

176

Hira with a vision for his people. But then he was beset by intense doubts and fears that his vision was the work of evil spirits. Only with the help of a close friend and with heroic personal effort was he able to conquer his doubts.[5] In fact, the predictable fall from vision is not just experienced once and for all. As the vision grows in power and influence, so grow the influences that would tear it down. The deaths of the crucified and burned saints are a measure of the power of their purpose.

When one has tumbled into the swamps of despair, all life is perceived through its murky depths. One tends not to see that there are also times of clarity and illumination. How easily we forget our highs! How eagerly we embrace our lows! And all the while we know that life is naturally experienced in rhythms and cycles, that every ascent is followed by a descent, even as day follows night. Perhaps it is nostalgia that tricks us, remembering the high with such an ache in our hearts that we cannot tolerate the present. "Nostalgia is the enemy of the warrior," said one of our teachers, which is just another way of saying, "The one who truly performs his vision does not cling to the past." Vision is an evolving kind of practical behavior. It cannot unfold by holding tight to some past visionary moment like a drowning man to a life preserver. Far better to let the moment slide into the hunger of our unconscious. Powers that shape the bringing forth of change lurk down there.

The fact that a person had a vision of the Sacred Mountains will not save him when the I.R.S. comes knocking on his door, or when he comes home early to find his wife in bed with another man. What may save him is what that moment in time has become, now that it has grown in him as only the past can grow, long after it is forgotten. For the vision to grow, it must be pressed down (depressed) into the depths of the unconscious, where the visionary seed is fertilized. He cannot be incorporated into the whole body of his vision with his head in the clouds. He must allow that bright, eternal moment to sink into the darkness of roots and forgotten, tangled things, and look to the practical present.

Jumping Mouse's journey to the Sacred Mountains is not merely outward, toward physical objectives, but inward, toward self-realization and transformation. In a psychological sense, he is in the process of changing his personal and social identity. The depression is an important step in individuation. The first big crisis after he returns will establish whether or not he is sufficiently motivated to carry through with what he saw down at the river. But there will be other crises. Some say the greater the obstacles, the greater the vision's power. If all goes well, the initiate will engage the monsters of the new life with weapons wrested from his threshold trial.

The modern initiate suffers more or less the same fate as Jumping Mouse. His people do not want the gifts he brings back from the Sacred River. They do not honor what he has done, or support his attempts to make his vision real. How can the vision be for his people when his people don't give a damn? Whether they like it or not, the vision was given to them. Whether they like it or not, they were there in spirit when our hero jumped and saw the Sacred Mountains. They too saw the source of the roaring in their ears. So what if they have forgotten it ever happened? Before his journey is done, Jumping Mouse will give the best of himself so that they can remember.

Profiles
in Incorporation

Jumping Mouse Went to the Edge of the Place of Mice and Looked out onto the Prairie. He looked up for Eagles. The Sky was Full of many Spots, each One an Eagle. But he was Determined to Go to the Sacred Mountains. He Gathered All of his Courage and Ran just as Fast as he Could onto the Prairie. His little Heart Pounded with Excitement and Fear.

—Storm, *Seven Arrows*

As time passes, Jumping Mouse cannot resist the need to make his way to the visionary mountains. Though he cannot know the length, breadth, and volume of his journey, he can take the first step. He's not getting any younger. He could indulge himself in a thousand diversions and *almost* deaden the roaring of the Sacred River at the back of his head. He can think, "I'm not strong enough," and *almost* persuade himself to wait until he is more prepared to tackle the monsters that hide in the shadows of tomorrow. If he is worthy of his vision, however, he will finally set out, in perfect innocence and trust, for the Sacred Mountains. "Therefore do not wait for great strength before setting out, for immobility will weaken you further. Do not wait to see very clearly before starting: One has to walk toward the light. Have you strength enough to take this first step?" (Philippe Vernier).

If he is not worthy of his vision, he will be swept away on the floodtide of a life he had hoped to leave behind. Though he may never cease to hear the roaring of the Sacred River, though he may forever revere his place of power, he will be forever haunted by the unawakened potency of what might have been.

The incorporation of the quester ends when he has reached the Sacred Mountains. Any other consummation is but an interlude on the path to his life goal. No wonder he can never be happy cooling his heels in Mouseland. He didn't return to an ending. He came back to a beginning. There is so much to do. He doesn't have time to sit around and try to prove that he has taken a swim in the Sacred

River. If they don't believe him that is their problem. His problem, on the other hand, has to do with getting to the shining mountains.

There are no meter sticks with which to measure the initiate's success or failure to negotiate his labyrinthine way to the culmination of his vision. The growth rate of vision is relative to the individual who pursues it. Hence, it is difficult, if not impossible, to evaluate therapeutic benefits with standardized evaluative instruments. We did try once, with a well-known "self-concept scale." The results showed "positive, persistent shifts in personal values and self-image." But we were evaluating returnees with stereotyped methods endemic in a mechanistic culture. Really, how does one evaluate Jumping Mouse's journey to the Sacred Mountains? The truest evaluation might be a simple circle, with a dot in the middle to represent the pilgrim.

The truth is, the wilderness quest is the briefest of metaphors for the candidate's visionary journey, a fleeting opportunity to jump and see life's desire shining in the distance. When it's done, the memory wanes. It *must* wane! Jumping Mouse cannot live in the past. He must go to the edge of the prairie of the present, trembling at the brink of its awesome dangers. Then he must set forth, trusting his frail bones to the rigors of the quest. All he has is a tiny, beating heart—but that is enough to make it all the way to the shining mountains.

Running Across the Prairie

There is a rule of thumb by which one can predict the relative success or failure of an incorporating quester to bring himself finally to the consummation of his vision. This measurement is not found in the Tennessee Self-Concept Scale or the Minnesota Multiphasic. It is found in the story of Jumping Mouse's heroic journey to the Sacred Mountains.

As the story goes, our hero shook the smog of Mouseland from his fur and took off across the great, unknown prairie. Beneath a merciless sky splotched by deadly eagles' shadows he ran, until he came to a sage bush. An old Mouse lived there, protected from the prairie and sustained by endless piles of seeds and other good things to eat. Old Mouse was willing to admit that the Sacred River existed, but he tried to discourage Jumping Mouse from seeking the Sacred Mountains. "They are only a myth," he said, inviting Jumping Mouse to stay with him under the sage bush where they could lead a comfortable, insulated life.

Jumping Mouse was astonished that Old Mouse did not know about the medicine of the great mountains. Though the elder mouse told him he would be a fool to leave, he declined to remain with his host. He ventured onto the prairie again. "The Ground was Rough. But he Arched his Tail and Ran with All his Might. He could Feel the Shadows of the Spots upon his Back as he Ran. All those Spots!"

Finally, he came to a stand of chokecherries. Everything he might need to prosper forever was there. "He could hardly Believe his Eyes." But his investigations were interrupted by the sound of labored breathing. A great buffalo lay in the shade. Jumping Mouse overcame his fear and approached the magnificent beast. "Why are you lying here?" he asked. "I am Sick and I am Dying," the buffalo answered, "and my Medicine has Told me that only the Eye of a Mouse can Heal me."

Understandably, Jumping Mouse was shocked and scared. "One of my Eyes! . . . One of my Tiny Eyes." But it was obvious the great soul was fading. "He will die," our hero realized, "if I do not Give him My Eye. He is too Great a Being to Let Die."

He told the sick buffalo that he could not let him die. He offered him one of his eyes. Straightaway, his "Eye Flew Out of his Head and the Buffalo was Made Whole." The buffalo jumped up and declared: "I know of your quest for the Sacred Mountains and of your Visit to the River. You have Given me Life so that I may Give-Away to the People. I will be your Brother Forever. Run under my Belly and I will Take you right to the Foot of the Sacred Mountains, and you need not Fear the Spots. The Eagles cannot See you while you run under Me. All they will See will be the Back of Buffalo."

Little Jumping Mouse gratefully accepted the buffalo's offer to run under his thundering hooves to the foot of the Sacred Mountains. It was frightening, running with only one eye, beneath hooves that could kill him with one misstep. But the buffalo reassured him: "My Way of Walking is the Sun Dance Way, and I Always Know where my Hooves will Fall." In time they reached their destination. The buffalo left Jumping Mouse at the foot of the Sacred Mountains.

The story of Jumping Mouse's journey contains the formula for reaching the mountains of vision. The prairie is the quester's life, his life span, the horizon he has to meet, the terms of the passage he must complete. This great prairie exists within him as well. In a very real sense he does not have to leave Mouseland in order to run across the prairie. He could spend the rest of his life in Mouseland and still the prairie would reach ahead of him; still the shadow of eagles would stalk him. These eagle spots in the sky are his fears, his monsters, the little deaths he faces ("Look at all those spots!"), any one of which could swoop down and get him, and that would be the end.

Old Mouse's spacious nest beneath the sage is not the prairie. Like Mouseland, it offers a false sense of security. It is, however, a landmark along Jumping Mouse's way. Breaking away from the cultivated mediocrity of Mouseland, daring to risk, he discovers that there is more to life than his home town. His passage to a new life is going fine—and this new place with its alternative lifestyle is proof. Now he knows more than the majority of his brothers and sisters. If he wants to, he can become a mouse of power, wealth, and influence. But he also knows that if he stays here he will become like the old Mouse, holding his snoot in the air and acting as though he has some superior knowledge, passing off his complacency, cynicism, and fear of risk as the truth: "I am Afraid that the Great Mountains are only a Myth. Forget your Passion to See Them and Stay here with me. . . ."

Giving Away an Eye

If the initiate is to fulfill his life's dream, he must venture beyond the nest of old Mouse. He must leave this refuge of stagnant know-it-all-ness and risk his life on the prairie. The success of his incorporation depends on these three steps: First, he must leave Mouseland and take on his fears (the shadow spots). Second, he must not be taken in by his initial success (old Mouse's nest). Third, he must give away an eye.

Anyone "performing the vision on earth for the people to see" comes eventually to the dying place of his ailing people. Confronting incontrovertable evidence of their plight, he gives away (sacrifices) an infinitely precious part of himself that they (as symbolized by the dying buffalo) may become well. The eye given away can be almost anything of great value: personal freedom, youth, affluence, love, fondest dreams. He voluntarily turns away from a normal life; he takes on a burden; he suffers a wounding; he dedicates his life to a higher calling. The decision comes from his deepest commitment of love for his people.

The giveaway is not without its rewards. Though he is half blind, the quester has earned a kind of protection from harm. The buffalo will shield him from the piercing eagles. He will journey to the great mountains beneath the broad, sheltering back of his people. The giveaway is the touchstone, the secret for attaining the Sacred Mountains. Failure would have quickly overwhelmed one who was not defending himself with love. "Putting on the whole armor of God" means giving away an eye so that the people may live.

"But surely," protests the rabid cynic, "it's all fine and good to wax optimistic about the giveaway of love, but in the modern analysis it is not so simple. We give away to the people and the people don't care, or they misunderstand our motives, or we misunderstand theirs. Let's face the facts. Everyone has his own self-interest at heart. Nowadays Jumping Mouse could be murdered en route to the Sacred River by a toad with a poisoned mind. He could die of leukemia or AIDS before he ever made it out of Mouseland. The Sacred River is polluted and the Sacred Mountains are being washed away by radioactive rain. What kind of foolishness is this, to say, with naïve conviction, that the way to visionary fulfillment is to give an eye away to the people? All you get is a half-blind Mouse."

Dark as the prairie may seem, the bargain with buffalo holds true. Consider the value of an eye. Consider the value of what we must part with before we die. Viewed from the perspective of modern life, the journey teems with shadow spots. Constant fear of them will erode our bodies from our spirits like print from a page. Our bones will become brittle. Our blood will slow. Eventually one of the spots will get us. *However* we arrive at our destination, in a Cadillac or on a cane, we will give away more than the symbolic eye. We will give away all, whether we want to or not.

The cynic is himself blind if he thinks there are better ways to reach the Sacred Mountains. Let him try going it alone, without the protective shielding of love. He will arrive at his destination pecked full of eagle holes. He will have given his pound of flesh, and none of it willingly. His mountains will not be bright and compelling. They will be black and ugly and he will be sorry he ever reached them. He will curse God, or his luck, and die.

The Modern Pilgrimage to the Sacred Mountains

Invariably, we measure an individual's progress through the life-long incorporation phase by the quality of his giveaway. We note whether he ever decides to leave Mouseland and risk his life among the shadow spots on the prairie. We watch him arrive at old Mouse's place and note whether he resolves to go on or to remain above or apart from his quest. We wonder what he will do with the newly realized power of an expanded purpose circle. Will he persist in his conviction that the Sacred Mountains are real and ultimately attainable? If so, he will accept the challenge of healing his people.

A letter received from a vision quester three years after he returned from the threshold clearly follows the drift of the Jumping Mouse story. A thirty-seven-year-old psychiatrist, husband, and father, Erroll had fasted for three days and nights in Death Valley.

> I came home excited, positive, and full of spirit. What I had not prepared for was the impending intensity of the incorporation period—which turned out to be my VISION QUEST. I found myself faced with all the boxes I had created for myself; father, husband, money earner, therapist, home keeper-upper, friend, etc., and it felt like none of them were really me. My spirit was too big to be confined in the narrow realities of my life.

Jumping Mouse returned home. He confronted all the roles he played in Mouseland. They paled beside the greatness of Self he had experienced in the desert. He felt apart, a stranger to the narrow realities of his life.

So I resisted. It was hard to be here and hard to work. I resented my life, but I also could see no alternative to escape it. I had, and chose, the responsibility of loving and caring for all that I was connected to.

He made the decision to start out across the great prairie of his life. He did this by renewing his commitment to his chosen life path, but there were shadow spots everywhere.

I was in a middle place, trapped between realities for about six weeks, with a fairly heavy, depressed feeling. Fortunately, I love life enough that I never considered giving up the struggle. But I felt stuck.

Thoughts of giving up are of old Mouse's nest of seeds, based on the belief that there are no Sacred Mountains. Therefore, one may despair of ever getting there. For a short while, Jumping Mouse succumbed to the paralysis of old Mouse's cynical den, torn between the "reality" of the Sacred River and the "myth" of the journey to the Sacred Mountains. Then he remembered that he had seen those mountains with his own eyes. They were no myth. He took off across the prairie again, running with his tail arched.

After a long time, I began to experience a deep inner feeling that my quest was to find a home for the bigness of my desert spirit in the expanses of my everyday life, that my vision quest was not to go away from my life but to come back into it as an adventure. It was as if I had been severed long ago, when I was born, and that life itself was my transition. This life transition is much harder than being alone on the desert. Intuitively, I sensed a future incorporation that was my true coming home— but that coming home depended upon the quality of my loving here in everyday life.

Erroll came to the dying place of the buffalo. He understood that he must give an eye away to his people.

So I renewed my commitment to my life, let go, merged into what is in each moment of my life but without the feeling of those experiences being in boxes. They were now opportunities to love, to seek, to quest, to be, to support, to connect to the Great Spirit all around me, in others and within me.

This has continued to the present.

Now our hero runs under the thundering hooves of those he loves. The vast prairie stretches before him. He is making his way to the mountains of vision.

Tales of Incorporation

The following stories illustrate various aspects of the modern quester's journey to the Sacred Mountains. They are but motes in the immensity of possible experiences. Nevertheless, each tale is instructive, contributing to a profile of the incorporation process as seen from the standpoint of the giveaway. For obvious reasons, certain names, places, dates, and other facts have been altered.

Paul (Midlife Crisis)

A thirty-nine-year-old husband and father of three children, Paul was spending less time at home. His job as a high school teacher seemed to satisfy him no more than his marriage. He had a brief affair with another woman. Guilt forced him to break it off. He went into a prolonged period of depression and began to drink too much.

At this point he enrolled in a wilderness fasting rite to celebrate his passage into middle age. He assessed his life situation. Was it really possible to continue with his wife and family, or had he passed the point of no return? Could he be satisfied with his work or did he need to change his occupation? What did he really want to do with his life?

He returned from the wilderness threshold whooping and hollering like a little boy. But he'd not had an easy time. Much of his fast had been spent curled up in his sleeping bag, wishing it were over, longing to be with his wife and kids. Nevertheless, questions had been answered. He could not conceive of a life without his family. He could also envision innovative ways to challenge his students. He returned home buoyed by glorious hopes.

Within a week, he hit rock bottom. Trying to reconnect with his wife, he uncovered old wounds. Anger flared up between them. He started drinking again, a fact which incited open rebellion among his children. The day-to-day demands of teaching smothered his attempts to be creative. It seemed to him that things had gone from bad to worse.

The crisis catalyzed the family to seek counseling. They began a long, gradual dance toward reconciliation. Sometimes the going got rough, and it was all Paul could do to pull his body free from the bed every morning. Somehow he held on. He gave up his fantasies of marital freedom and concentrated his energies toward giving away an eye to his people. He slacked off on his drinking, earning himself a new respect. He changed his style of teaching, worrying less about whether or not he was covering the textbook. Slowly the family came through a dark time.

But something was missing and he couldn't quite put his finger on it. There was something else he had to do with his life, some kind of mark to leave on the pages of personal history. He went into the fasting mountains a second time, experiencing none of his previous difficulties, and returning with a crazy idea about what he could do to alter and enrich his life, and to fuel his craving to give away to the people of his town. His plans gestated for nearly a year before he took the first step, volunteering to serve on the Independence Day parade committee. Two years later, he became the "parade master."

Nowadays, people travel many a mile to view one of the finest parades a small community of twenty-five thousand can offer, a whacky, wonderful, joyous spectacle, involving everyone in the community, from babies to elders. And still the parade grows in size and spirit. There is nothing quite like it anywhere else on earth.

Carol (Passing into Adulthood)

A nineteen-year-old college freshman, Carol was the eldest in a Mormon family of four children. Though the idea was disturbing to her parents, she was determined to participate in a wilderness passage rite. She knew they harbored fears that she would fall away from the Church and be lost in the outer darkness reserved for those who reject the light.

Her parents were right about her. She was seriously considering becoming an ex-Mormon. When she went alone and fasted in the

White Mountains, she also marked her decision to leave the Church. She stood on a rock ledge overlooking a dramatic two-thousand-foot drop into the alkali mirror of Deep Springs Lake. Obeying the impulse of a dream she'd had the night before, she picked up a stone to represent her Mormon childhood. Then she threw the stone into the abyss. Plummeting in a flat arc, the stone disappeared into the deep distance. As it fell, she had the distinct feeling it was she who was falling to her death, forsaken by the saints and angels of the Church. She never heard it land.

Returning home, she hinted to her father, the more liberal parent, about what she had done. His reaction persuaded her not to go into detail.

Soon after, she went back to college on the East Coast. She met a man several years older and fell in love. He took her virginity and, shortly thereafter, left her for another. Raised with traditional values, she was deeply hurt by this experience. She carried the pangs around until the summer, when she enrolled in an underworld journey of six days and nights without food or companionship.

She returned from the threshold having put an end to her grieving over the love affair. She had decided to give herself to studies leading to formal certification as a midwife. Returning to her family home for a visit, she found her parents in the midst of crisis. Her father had fallen in love with another woman and was leaving her mother. Carol stayed with the shattered family until it was time to go back to school.

Currently she is a senior in college, majoring in disciplines pertinent to midwifery. As childhood friends have dropped away she has made many new ones. She has not joined an organized body of believers in any particular faith, though her spirituality grows. She wrote to tell us she had fallen in love again, this time with a woman.

David (Life-Threatening Illness)

A divorced father in his early forties, David lost a kidney and seriously impaired the function of the other when he was almost killed in an automobile accident. Medical experts told him he had ten years before renal failure. An active man, the director of a "think tank," he refused to accept the doctors' verdict. He read every book he could get his hands on and became an expert on the function and health of the human kidney. He placed himself on a saltless vegetarian diet and a disciplined regimen of physical exercise and daily meditation—and kept working.

Soon after his accident, he met Roxanne, a younger woman, and the two grew to love each other. Roxanne urged him to explore alternatives to modern medicine as a means of healing the remaining kidney. He went to healers, acupuncturists, body therapists, and finally, one day, he enrolled in a wilderness passage rite.

Though his medical advisors recommended against it, he fasted in the desert for four days and nights, rinsing his kidney out with a gallon of water per day. It was the middle of winter. The last night of his trial, cold winds blew from the north and sleet slanted down like bullets. He prayed for healing, for his children, and for Roxanne, who was fasting half a mile away.

When he came in the next morning he looked tired but healthy. No, he had experienced little trouble with his kidney. He felt in good health. He had received assurances from the spirits to whom he prayed that he could control the breakdown of his kidney and extend his lifetime. He returned to a vigorous work schedule, flying all over the country to consult with clients and make presentations. After a few months, he found blood in his urine and began to have back pains, signals that his kidney was acting up again.

He curtailed his work schedule, convinced he had to concentrate more of his energy on bodily health. This gave him more time to be with Roxanne, who loved him with healing insight and passion. Further medical assessment revealed that his kidney was in no worse condition than it had been a year before. He decided to go on another wilderness fast.

With this second fast his sense of his own ability to heal himself grew. He claimed that when he surrendered to the influence of nature, he could sense his immune system tingling around him, invigorated by the natural medicine of stars, wind, and growing things. His power song was ragged and passionate, like the scream of an eagle. It clung to the darkness of his fear like sparks of fire.

When he returned, he initiated a two-year plan ending in semiretirement, convinced that work-related stress damaged his kidney. Occasionally, the organ sent him a twinge, just to let him know it was still there. Generally, trouble signs decreased. He continued his diet and exercises, spending more time with Roxanne outdoors near their home.

When he resigned the directorship of the think tank, Roxanne and he decided to celebrate with a "graduation exercise": a six-day underworld journey through the high desert. The two walked separate courses through biting winds and freezing nights. Snow that fell the first day stayed frozen on the ground for the remainder of the journey. The last night was the coldest. Water bottles were frozen by midnight. It was so cold a pack rat climbed into our truck and made a nest on the engine block next to the carbureter.

At first light a loud voice jolted us from our dreams of endless summer. We poked our noses into the frosty air. Who could that be at this purgatorial hour, singing at the top of his lungs? David burst into the frozen stillness of our camp, a gaunt, grizzled animal, howling with life and laughter. Shivering and protesting, we pulled our clothes on like a couple of tenderfeet and howled back at him.

David healed himself. His kidney has not deteriorated appreciably in the past five years. In the meantime, Roxanne and he traveled extensively in Mexico and Central America, becoming intimately acquainted with the social plight of the people there. They returned to America for a brief stay, and then returned to live in Nicaragua, where they teach educators how to utilize videotape techniques in the classroom.

Raymond (Retirement)

A San Francisco attorney in his early seventies, Raymond participated in a passage rite at the urging of his son Brian, who had fasted the year before. At the preparatory meetings he reminisced about his life, his ongoing love for his wife, the trials and tribulations of raising three sons, and his love for his work. It had not been easy, but it was worth every second, he said, charming everyone with his optimistic acceptance of the aging process. He was like a good wine, sweet with wisdom, tart with insight.

"I'm tired of working," he said. "I've got to let the business go, let the younger guys take over." He admitted that he found it hard to retire, not that he hadn't been planning to do so for many years. He might have been tired, but his love for his work gleamed in his wrinkled face. He had reason to be proud. His firm had a history of taking up the causes of minorities: blacks, Hispanics, Jews, gay people, and others. Even at the age of seventy-four, his social conscience kept him abreast of every movement, every controversy. Indeed, it would be difficult for this battered old counselor to withdraw from the ring. Nevertheless, he said, "I'm determined to celebrate my passage into retirement."

He fasted alone for four days and nights in a canyon in the Eureka Valley, a canyon we called Old Dad Canyon, after Steven Foster's father. His son, Brian, fasted with him, claiming the upper reaches of the same canyon. Midway between them was a small spring, the only water for miles around. We never saw either of them until the morning they were due to come out. We half expected a man of Raymond's age to take it easy on himself and come in early. But there he was, toiling toward us in the distance, his son at his side.

As it turned out, he thoroughly enjoyed himself, experiencing no ill effects from fasting. He had chosen a wide bend in the canyon, a terrace with a huge boulder for shelter and shade. Each day he trudged up the canyon to the spring, where he checked the stone-pile and left a sign for Brian that he was OK. This he particularly enjoyed, savoring the memories of taking Brian, just a youngster, camping in the High Sierra. No, he hadn't thought much about death, having had too much fun just being alive and alone, without responsibilities. Yes, he had thought about his retirement. He had performed a small fire ceremony where he said goodbye to the firm. Mostly, he seemed to be living in the present, relaxed, happy, and self-possessed. He returned filled with ideas on how, in his greater years, he could help those less fortunate than himself.

After returning home it took him two years actually to take the step and officially retire. Even then, he kept his finger in the pie, advising, consulting, even making court appearances now and then. Ever so reluctantly, he let go, and turned his attention to the final years prefacing his death.

Trent (Burglary)

Almost eighteen, Trent was headed for juvenile hall for a series of burglaries. The oldest son in a fatherless family of four, he had been caught at such shenanigans before. He seemed to be a nice kid, and was deeply devoted to his mother. Nobody wanted to see him wind up in jail. His mother pled his cause to his probation officer. The officer pled his cause before the juvenile judge. The judge reasoned that something drastic should be done and gave Trent a "no choice": Go to juvenile hall, or enroll in a wilderness passage rite and return to a year's probation. Of course, the miscreant chose the fast. Anything but juvenile hall.

It seemed to us the real problem was not burglary, but Trent's relationship to his mother, who called us repeatedly, her voice filled with anxiety and concern over her son's well-being in the wilderness without food or company. "Don't worry, mom, I'll be all right," he boasted, putting on a brave look. He seemed to bask in her concern. Tattooed on his wrist was a heart pierced by a dagger. The heart read "MOM."

During his three-day fast he paced all over the Grapevine Mountains like a caged lion. Several times he was spied looking down at basecamp from a nearby cliff. One moonless night we were certain we heard him descending a dangerous slope. We called out to him but got no answer.

When it was over he certainly looked better than he did before he went in. The sun had turned his pallor to a tan and his self-conscious swagger was almost gone. He told us he wasn't afraid of the dark anymore. And in the name of his sainted mother he swore he would never steal again or be a burden to her.

Two months later a patrolman caught him red-handed one night, burglarizing a home in an expensive part of Marin County. By then he was eighteen. There was nothing anybody could do. He went to jail. When he got out, he disappeared. Nobody heard from him for nearly a year. Meanwhile, there was a rash of cat burglaries that bore his mark. Surveillance was intensified and he was finally apprehended. He had been hiding out in a lean-to on the thickly forested slopes of Mt. Tamalpais, every once in a while visiting his mother to get needed supplies.

Loraine (On a Shamanic Journey)

A thirty-six-year-old wife and mother of two children, from a fashionable suburb of Oakland, Loraine enrolled in a wilderness fasting rite after being told to by "guiding spirits." The spirits had come to her while she was participating in a workshop run by a Bay Area shaman. "Pray to the four grandfathers, dance on a rock, and bury your rattle in a sacred place," was the charge given her by the spirits. This she was determined to do, regardless of obstacles, during her threshold fast.

During the preparatory phase, Loraine was reticent about her personal life, refusing, in fact, to discuss it, impatient with questions about her relationship to husband and children. She had come to do what her "guiding spirits" had told her to do. She held herself apart from the preparations of others in the group, considering her own objectives to be more sacred than theirs. Although she was warned that the fasting rite might be quite different from what she imagined it to be, she listened with one ear, preferring to obey her "guiding spirits" about how to prepare, making cunning little prayer arrows and beaded feathers for purposes of ceremony.

Reluctantly, we let her go into a threshold fast in the mountains ringing the Eureka Valley. On the third day of a four-day fast she returned to basecamp, limping weakly, her cheeks streaked with tears. She said she was sick, that the weather had been too hot, that the ground had been too stony, that the soil was too dusty, that her water bottle smelled, that she was sure she had heard a rattlesnake rattling near her place. She sat down by her pack, being careful first to lay down her ensolite pad so that she could sit on it and not get her jeans dirty.

We asked her if she had done what her "guiding spirits" had told her to do. "No!" she wailed. "I didn't do any of it!" "Then what did you do?" we asked. "I lay in my sleeping bag and looked up at a little patch of blue sky. I didn't feel like doing anything else." "You didn't pray to the grandfathers, dance on a rock, or bury your rattle?" "No!" she scoffed. "This is no shamanic experience! And I've had my fill of the desert!"

In time, Loraine was able to look at her behavior. In the elders' council she listened to the "success stories" of the others in the group and realized she hadn't been ready to tackle such an ordeal as a four-day fast. She saw how she had suckered herself into a negative reaction, how she had lured herself into a shadow place with naive expectations. Anger flashed, anger at men, anger at her husband, anger at her life situation, anger at her secure little world in upper-class Oakland. The real crisis of her life reared its spectral head, her midlife crisis, her deepest fears that life would amount to nothing.

She promised to return, to attempt the fast a second time, to accept its harsh conditions. That was three years ago. We haven't heard from her since.

Susan (Passing into Adulthood)

A seventeen-year-old girl from a divorced family, Susan came back before her trial was over. She said she had been unable to find a good place to sleep.

It was easy to see that her inability to find a place mirrored her home life up to that time. Shunted back and forth among mother, father, and grandparents, she had begun to dislike all her homes. She had taken to the streets where she got into trouble. We had met her in a continuation high school, where she was barely holding on.

It was her sense of being victimized by her environment that concerned us. She could not find a place to sleep because everywhere the ground was too hard, the rocks too sharp, the pine needles too sticky. We might have wished that, like a burr seed, she had landed somewhere and clung, asserting her strength at least to hold on. But how can Jumping Mouse return to a home that never existed? The rocks are too sharp, the ground too hard and cold.

Susan went back to her father's house, but apparently he could have cared less, absorbed in the pursuit of his own pleasure. She took to the streets again and met an older man who asked her to come and live with him. She agreed and quit school. They started living together in Oakland. She found out he was a junkie. It was not long before she was one, too.

Tom (Cocaine Addiction)

Tom graduated from high school with honors and the vote of fellow students as "most likely to succeed." But success has its own schedule. He enrolled in a community college. He did well, but his heart was not in it. Raised in a sheltered home, he had a yen to find out what he did not know. He cut his course load and got a part-time job in a clothing store. Within a year, he was offered the position of manager. He quit school and started working full-time. Before long he had built up capital. The store flourished and expanded. He bought a new car and hung out with his business friends. They introduced him to cocaine, for which he developed a daily craving.

196

To feed his addiction, Tom began to deal. Soon he had amassed a small fortune, a traumatized sinus, a slowly deteriorating nervous system, a profound self-loathing, and a life of paranoia. He knew he was up the river without a paddle. The opportunity to change came when he was busted for dealing. The judge, who could have thrown the book at him, recognized his potential. He was placed on three years' probation as a convicted felon. The sentence mandated that he enter some sort of rehabilitative program. He chose the passage rite.

After four days and nights alone in Death Valley, he returned in the eddies of a fresh breeze, relaxed and ready to get on with his life. He had ceremonially buried his coke spoon somewhere in a rocky wash, to be unearthed by future archeologists looking for artifacts. He declared he'd had a vision. He was going to be a lawyer.

His incorporation was marked by the classic actions of successful self-rehabilitation. He sold his clothing business and moved to another city, thus cutting himself off from his cocaine habitat. He enrolled in a state university. He made new friends and kept his grades up. When his probation ended, he applied to law school. He was accepted.

Mary (Sexually Abused as a Child)

Mary, aged thirty, entered a group counseling program for sexually abused women to explore the pervasive and devastating effects her father's repeated attacks had had on her childhood and later life. As a married woman, the mother of two children, she had come to a crisis point. She had to be relieved of these crushing memories. Though she had confronted her father with the truth, he had denied everything. After that, she resolved to hate him with the revenge of forever. But this hatred itself symbolized the kind of power he still held over her. She could not forget him, even when making love with her husband. He haunted her every attempt to forget him.

When she enrolled in the fasting rite, she said, "As long as I hold this hatred for my father I will be victimized by him." She knew that the hurt and confused little girl was somehow going to have to heal herself without her father's help. Before the trail ended, she would attempt to wash herself clean of bitterness. She would say goodbye to her father, and die. The person who emerged from her purpose circle would be oriented to the promise of the future.

She returned from the threshold with pain lines etched in her face. The fast had not been easy. She had thrown up twice and had experienced a great deal of bodily malaise. She had been so weak she could hardly make it to the stonepile to check on her buddy. Many times she thought about giving up. Repeatedly, she wrestled with the ghost of her father, unable to forgive his refusal to confess. Finally, the last night, she burned her father in a small purpose circle fire, changing his face via the purifying element to that of a stranger. She saw him as a sick man, a weak and guilty man who was no longer her father. Then she was able to forgive him.

Eagerly she embraced her family. For a while, her love life improved, as did communication with her husband. But then came the predictable fall. Her husband said something that made her feel vulnerable and betrayed. She curled up inside, as was her habit, and wrestled with her father again. He had not given up after the knockout in the first round.

Her depression finally resolved itself into the commitment she had made in the desert. The burning issue was still: "Goodbye stranger. I forgave you. I died for those memories. Now I'm going on with my life." This commitment carried her through several years of a rocky, but gradually improving love life.

She continued to work at the agency for abused children and women. With an ever-deepening commitment to her people, she is healing herself. She takes women with childhood abuses similar to hers on excursions into the wilderness, where they use Mother Earth's influences to purge their bodies and stanch their wounds.

Mark (Passing into Adulthood)

A confident, intense eighteen-year-old high school graduate, Mark returned from the wilderness trial in high spirits and with gratitude to his parents, who, he said, had prepared him well. He talked about his experiences openly and freely, but seemed more interested in what he was returning to: a summer job and then travel overseas (his parents' graduation present).

Two weeks later in the elders' circle, he seemed no less enthusiastic about his future. He had plans for college when he got back from Europe. He would study ecobiology and volunteer for the Peace Corps in some distant country. When questioned about his threshold experience, he showed high levels of understanding and insight. Yes, he had been afraid. It had been hard to fast. He had conquered his fears by observing himself. What vision did he bring back for his people? His energy, his wits, and the desire to be of use to humankind. Would he ever want to fast again? "Maybe. But there are other challenges to face," he said. "I'm prepared to face them."

He went traveling in Europe, most of the time by himself. When he returned, he enrolled at the University of California at Santa Cruz. He majored in environmental education. When he graduated he joined the Peace Corps, and is now serving in Tanzania.

Diana (Passing into Adulthood with a Mystical Vision)
A seventeen-year-old "A" student from a local Marin County high school, Diana was given a great gift. On the last night in her purpose circle, the following happened:

> I looked at the moon—a glowing crescent. I actually saw a pure, shining dove rise out of it and descend to Earth! I had my eyes wide open. I saw that beautiful bird flying down toward the planet. I closed my eyes and screamed: "Dear Father, We need!" I thought that the image was a hallucination. I was afraid to believe in such a powerful sight.
>
> Then it clicked. I was sitting there in my bag in the blackness. My head was tilted up toward the sky and stars, and my eyes were closed. I began to feel raindrops on my closed eyelids. Then, still with my eyes shut, I saw triangular, no, pyramid-shaped figures of light traveling from every direction, heading through my eyes into my soul. I felt a surge of power, of awareness.
>
> I opened my eyes. Those brilliant stars were still sending down pyramids of energy to me—I saw it all clearly. Like a river there was a constant flow of warmth, power, and light coming directly from the stars into my being, through my eyes.
>
> Everything just seemed to click. The Spirit (I call it God) sent me that mystical message: Love. He gave me that reason why I'm here on earth. This wonderful planet gives us the place not only to exist as a life form, but to grow together. I'm here

to participate in that potential fellowship. I'm here to Love and accept. Through these images—the stars, the sun, all this energy in the world—I can collect it within me, and direct it to humanity.

She called herself Glowing Mountain in the Dawn. But she could not glow on the top of her mountain for very long. She had to finish up her senior year and decide what to do with her life. Nobody at home was going to give her special attention just because she had a vision. There was no body of community elders to tell her she was specially favored with medicine power. All she had to go on was the memory, graven deep on her soul.

She carried on with her plans to go to college and enrolled at the University of Colorado. In her sophomore year she became involved with a dark-eyed, handsome man from Montana, a student in her English class. He was the man of her dreams. But he wanted her to drop out of school with him and go live in Montana. How could she do such a thing? Above all, she valued her education. Her parents, burdened with five children, were helping to put her through. How could she let them down?

Eric and the call of the wild gradually drew her into their spell. She dropped out of school and went to live in a rural town forty miles from Missoula. They lived together for a year while Eric worked for the forestry service and she waited on tables. The flush of romance faded. She began to wonder if she had made the right choice. After a series of crises, she left Eric and returned to the university.

Before a semester was gone she realized how much she missed her man. Her man, too, was not about to let her go. He drove down to visit her and they couldn't resist being together again. He wondered if he should quit his job and come to Boulder, maybe go back to school. Undecided, he had to return to work in Montana.

Soon after, Diana discovered she was pregnant. Fearfully, she wrote and told Eric. He wrote back saying he wanted her, and he wanted the baby. Still, she felt the unfairness of it. Why had it happened in the middle of her education? Why had she been chosen to bear this added burden? She accepted it, though, down in her heart. Years before, in the desert, a vision had told her that her mission in life was to *love*.

She went to live with Eric. The two were married in a simple but meaningful ceremony. A baby boy was born. Diana proved to be a good mother. There was always a certain balance, a centeredness, a down-to-earthness about her. She was never one of those gaunt, starved-looking mystics who mortified and clawed their way along the *via negativa* toward the Light of Lights. She ran across the prairie and came to the place of the buffalo. It was in her womb.

Hildegard (Midlife Transition)

She wrote us a letter postmarked Augsburg, West Germany, expressing, in halting English, the desire to enroll in a vision fast course at the School of Lost Borders. She described herself as a divorced woman of fifty-five, a mother of two sons, and a Jungian analyst whose specialty was children and family work. We enrolled her in a May course and in due time she showed up in our little redneck town at the edge of the Mojave, an elegant, cultured, beautiful woman radiating smiles and serious intent.

Prompted to talk a little about her personal history, she sketched in the rough outlines of her life story. Born in 1932 into a wealthy family living near Frankfurt, Hildegard had had no ordinary childhood, coinciding, as it did, with Hitler's rise to power. The youngest of four children, she was the only daughter, and, from the time she was six years old, her father, a weapons-tooling expert, had sexually abused her. Her mother, an ineffectual, otherworldly, Lutheran woman, had refused to look at what was going on, and Hildegard, pinned down by the threats of her father, had nowhere to turn, no one to tell.

When she was seven, the Nazis invaded Poland. By then, she was already accustomed to seeing *der Führer* in her home, where he frequently came to consult with her father, Heinrich, whose weapons empire included several munitions factories vital to the war effort. At such a young age, she was largely ignorant of what was happening in her country. Nazism and the vapid precepts of her mother's faith were the only values she knew. Sensitive, pretty, and intelligent, she was forced to experience at first hand the inhumanity of Nazism in her father's domineering and brutal treatment of her. Plagued by nightmares and fits of uncontrollable shaking, she sought surcease in the dark woods near her home, the only place where her violated heart and body could find healing and relief.

By 1942, the Allies had stepped up their bombing raids on the Frankfurt area, concentrating particularly on the huge factory run by Heinrich's corporation. Hildegard's life became a living nightmare of bombs, airplanes, antiaircraft guns, air-raid sirens, and shelters. In time, saturation bombing techniques were employed, not only against the factory, but against her father's ancestral estate. It became obvious to her that evil reigned supreme in the world, that men existed to make war, to make the local people disappear, to murder innocent women and children. Such feelings were intensified one day, as she was walking with her grandmother through the devastated streets of her home town. A P-51 Mustang appeared without warning and indiscriminately strafed the town. As the two of them ran for shelter, her grandmother was struck in the head by fragments from a cannon shell and died in her granddaughter's arms.

When the war ended, Heinrich went to prison, but the family business didn't die. Carried on by the sons, and the father who joined them two years later, tooling processes were adapted to peacetime uses and the enterprise flourished. By then, Hildegard was fifteen and attending the local *Gymnasium*. Later, from the University at Heidelberg, she earned advanced diplomas in music (she was an accomplished flutist) and Jungian psychoanalysis. After graduation, she met and married a professor of mathematics at the University of Munich and went to live with him in his country home near Augsburg. She bore the professor two sons before she was divorced from him in 1960. At that point, she went into an extended period of depression and required intense psychotherapy over a period of years. Unable to exorcise inner terrors created by her father and the war, especially the guilt-demon caused by her family's association with Hitler and the Nazi party, she severed connections with her parents and brothers and informed them that she wanted none of their money, including her multimillion-dollar share of her father's will.

As her anger against her father, other men, and her own birthright deepened, shadow monsters like self-contempt, sexual inadequacy, nightmare, paranoia, and suicidal ideation surfaced in her waking mind. But even as she did battle with them, she made the decision to be a private psychotherapist, to find a raison d'être in the giving of her attentive and sensitive mind to others who were also in crisis.

Twenty years later, in middle age, after a succession of lovers and a life of increasing success as a Jungian therapist, she slipped back into the swamps of depression, realizing she had never put the shadow monsters to rest. Their vengeful return coincided with her fifty-fifth birthday. All at once, her life seemed desperate, haunted, fearful, violent, cruel, and loveless. In the family's ancestral castle deep in the Black Forest, she sought refuge, reliving her girlhood love for the natural world, but spectres from the past leered from behind the trees. Everywhere she went the painful memory of her father was there. Fearing that she might go insane if she did not put his memory to rest along with his body, which had been buried years before, she wrote to a vision-fasting school in the California desert.

Hildegard fasted for four days and nights in the mountains north of the Eureka Valley. She had never seen the desert, let alone lived alone in it. The night before she crossed the threshold, the fearful little girl appeared, angry, stubborn, anxious. Nervously, but with a self-possessed courage, she set out for her fasting place the next morning. After four hot May days in the Eureka Valley, she returned the fifth morning, dirty, sweaty, burned the color of cedar bark, her green eyes dancing with her smile. "It went wery good!" she laughed, her face betraying what she'd learned about herself, something heroic, magical, and adamantine. She could have been mistaken for an ancient Celtic priestess, standing tall, her blond-grey hair burnished with dust and sunlight.

She returned to her home in Germany and sent us glowing letters about changes that had occurred in her life. She said she'd found a tiger inside herself strong enough to drive her father off, that she was using some of the vision fast techniques in her therapy with others, and that she wanted to enroll in an advanced training course and an underworld journey (six days walking without food in total solitude). Now that we knew her better, she seemed a likely candidate, a strong, intelligent, mature, professional woman, a quick and willing student. She could bring what she learned back to her people in Germany. "Yes," we answered. "Why don't you come back this spring?"

She spent an April and May with us in the northern Mojave desert, far from the Nazi ghosts stalking the land of her birth. The desert sun sublimed the dross from her body and psyche. She learned to trust herself listening to the wisdom voices of the wind, the juniper tree, the big sage brush, the mountain creek, the hard, blue sky. She walked at night by the light of the goddess moon and encountered the impassive rattlesnake hunting in the afterglow of day. She slept to the howls of coyote and the hoots of owl. She helped us help others to prepare and cross the threshold, prayed with us for their welfare, and aided in the incorporation process. She learned to see the mythology in the life story, the mirror surrounding the symbol. She put her dreams in the great circle of the six directions and saw that all things were in balance within herself, that her fits of depression, her shadow monsters, her childhood terrors were but necessary elements in the harmony of balance she danced every fleeting instant. She performed ceremony in her own way, with her own symbols, without a mediator or high priest standing between herself and that to which she prayed.

In May she embarked on her underworld journey, a twenty-five mile trek through the highlands of the Inyo Mountains. The first day of her journey led her up through a gorge as steep, dark, and trailless as anywhere she had ever been. We watched as her toiling form was swallowed by the shadows of a bend in the canyon. Ahead of her lay six days of fasting and walking, dancing with her shadows, seeking the story in the natural world that would answer her question: "Am I to do this work among my people in Germany?" In an hour the answer appeared—the skeletal remains of a mountain lion, lying directly across her path beneath a pinyon tree.

Although we monitored the checkpoints during the period she was alone, we never saw her. Attempts to track her for small distances revealed how lightly she walked upon the earth. She left small, neat notes reassuring us that she was all right.

The final morning, when she emerged, we saw her far off across the sagebrush meadow, walking strongly, a lilt to her step. The faint tones of a song she was singing hung upon the thin air, rising in intensity as she neared. It was Mozart. She walked into basecamp looking fresher and more fit that when she had left. Her embrace was solid and real. Her question had been answered. The mountain lion had walked in joy and balance.

Every spring since, she has come to our little town, bringing with her several of her compatriots. She takes them into the Inyo Mountains (translation: "dwelling place of the Great Spirit"), where they fast and live alone and seek answers to life questions besetting them. Because it is difficult to find such comparatively unspoiled wilderness in her homeland, she brings them here, to a desert land unknown in Germany, to the land of the former enemies of the Third Reich, the same land that spawned the airplane and the pilot that swooped in low, so long ago, and took the life of her grandmother.

9

The Sacred Mountains of Vision

*Suddenly he Ran upon a Gray Wolf who was Sitting
there doing absolutely Nothing.*

"Hello, Brother Wolf," Jumping Mouse said.

*The Wolf's Ears Came Alert and his Eyes Shone.
"Wolf! Wolf! Yes, that is what I am, I am a Wolf!"
But then his mind Dimmed again and it was not long
before he Sat Quietly again, completely without
Memory as to who he was. Each time Jumping Mouse
Reminded him who he was, he became Excited with the
News, but soon would Forget again.*

*"Such a Great Being," thought Jumping Mouse,
"but he has no Memory."*

*Jumping Mouse Went to the Center of this New
Place and was Quiet. He Listened for a very long time
to the Beating of his Heart. Then Suddenly he Made
up his Mind. He scurried back to where the Wolf Sat
and he Spoke.*

"Brother Wolf," Jumping Mouse said. . . .

"Wolf! Wolf!" said the Wolf.

*"Please, Brother Wolf," said Jumping Mouse.
"Please Listen to me. I Know what will Heal you. It
is One of my Eyes. And I Want to Give it to you.
You are a Greater Being than I. I am only a Mouse.
Please take it."*

*When Jumping Mouse Stopped Speaking his Eye
Flew out of his Head and the Wolf was made Whole.*

*Tears Fell down the Cheeks of Wolf, but his little
Brother could not See them. For Now he was Blind.*

*"You are a Great Brother," said the Wolf, "for
Now I have my Memory. But Now you are Blind. I
am the Guide into the Sacred Mountains. I will Take
you there. There is a Great Medicine Lake there. The*

most Beautiful Lake in the World. All the World is
Reflected there. The People, the Lodges of the People,
and All the Beings of the Prairies and Skies. "

—Storm, *Seven Arrows*

It all began when Mouse heard the roaring of the Sacred River in his ears. Innocently, he set out to investigate. That is where Raccoon came in. He took Mouse down to the River so that he could talk to Frog and get some jumping medicine. Now that you can see the full sweep of Jumping Mouse's life, you can appreciate how relatively minor, yet important, Raccoon's role was in his growth and development. If Raccoon had not been there, Jumping Mouse might never have made it down to the Sacred River, and if he had not gone to the river, how could he have seen the Sacred Mountains shining in the distance? If he had never seen the Sacred Mountains, how could he have realized he was dissatisfied with his old life in Mouseland? If he had not been dissatisfied, haunted by his vision of the great mountains, how could he have left the comfort and security of Mouseland and the only life he knew, to venture onto the dangerous prairie beneath the pitiless eye of Eagle? If he had not ventured out on the prairie, how could he have given an eye, healed his people, and gained safe conduct to the foot of the Sacred Mountains?

Jumping Mouse reached the threshold of his final life passage. But he was not through giving away. A forlorn wolf sat at the threshold, trying to remember who he was. Jumping Mouse realized he had one thing that would heal the wolf. He had come all this way across the prairie just to give away his other eye. The giving of it blinded him. The shining mountains of his vision were plunged into darkness.

Wolf, however, was healed. He remembered that he was the Guide to the Sacred Mountains. He led his blind benefactor to the Medicine Lake. Jumping Mouse drank from the lake and Wolf described its beauty to him. But soon it was time for Wolf to go. There were others coming to the Sacred Mountains. They also needed his guidance. Little Mouse was frightened to be alone. Now he was easy prey for the eagles.

> Jumping Mouse Sat there Trembling in Fear. It was no use Running, for he was Blind, but he Knew an Eagle would find him Here. He Felt a Shadow on his Back and Heard the Sound that Eagles Make. He Braced himself for the Shock. And the Eagle Hit! Jumping Mouse went to Sleep.

The mountains of vision were the mountains of death. Blind Jumping Mouse came to the end of his life. How long ago did Raccoon take him down to the Sacred River? How long ago did he jump as high as he was able and see these same mountains glowing in the distance? How could he have known what he was in for? How could he have known what the journey would cost him? Of course, by giving his eyes away he was able to make it all the way to the very heart of the mountains of vision, Medicine Lake.

Jumping Mouse didn't know it, but the wolf was a trickster. He would have had Jumping Mouse's eye whether it was given or not. For no one enters the Sacred Mountains unless he is blind. No one goes there unless it is time to die. No one reaches the source of their vision without being led there by the Lord of Death. And no one drinks from Medicine Lake unless he is ready to slake his thirst forever.

The little hero could no longer prolong the inevitable. He had come all this way just to be eagle-bait. Well, so be it. Trembling in fear, he waited for death's pounce.

The Two-Eyes Giveaway Dance

And everything comes to One,
As we dance on, dance on, dance on.
    —Theodore Roethke, "Once More, the Round"

The Jumping Mouse story is not bound by conventions of past, present, and future. On its deepest level the time framework is always Now. We are always hearing the roaring of the Sacred River in our ears. We are always leaving Mouseland in search of it. We are always scampering across the prairies of our lives. We are always challenged by the need to give away to our people. We are always at the gates of the visionary mountains of death. We are always blind eagle-bait.

And are we not always giving one eye to buffalo and one eye to wolf? One eye looks outward to love and the people. The other eye looks inward to death and illumination. Without the inward eye we would never meet eagle. Each is an inseparable part of our journey, the quality of which depends on our dancing with both eyes at the same time.

With our buffalo perception we love, trust, work, plan, and serve the people. With buffalo's eye we see beauty in others and are moved to compassion. We want to be with them, heal them, be yoked with them. Through this eye we apprehend the wisdom and order of the universe.

With our wolf perception we see into the shadow life of things, the fall, the changes, the dyings, and the deaths. Through the wolf's eye we walk into the Sacred Mountains and approach the Medicine Lake. He guides us to mystical illumination and spiritual transformation. Though blinded, we see.

Jumping Mouse's story illustrates this dual aspect of human perception. One eye is for light and the other is for darkness. One eye sees the sacred and the other the profane. One eye sees the outward show; the other eye sees what is behind the emperor's clothes. The vision that we seek to give away is not without its darker side, and the blindness that we enter is not without clarity of sight. The journey to the Sacred Mountains is dappled with light and shadow. The path through the sunny glade leads to the swamp of gangrene. The abyss of despair leads to the springs of healing. Illumination and blindness dwell as one in the reflected waters of Medicine Lake. Contradictions are resolved in the two-eyes dance.

The balancing of the two worlds, as symbolized by the two-eyes giveaway of Jumping Mouse, is the task of the visionary journey. The world of the threshold, the sacred, natural world, must be weighed against the profane, gross, secular world. The apparent contradiction of spiritual and material must be balanced and integrated. The sanctified and the obscene, the saint and the sinner, the

212

innocent and the experienced, the virgin and the whore, the pure and the mixed, are poised in the two-eyes dance.

The two-eyes giveaway extends to all dimensions of our experience, for we live between the human of ourselves (the buffalo) and the "nature" of ourselves (the wolf). Our circles of purpose comprehend male/female, emotional/intellectual, waking/dreaming, freedom/responsibility, young/old, inward/outward, and birth/death. As we journey, we learn that all contradictions, all forked paths, are resolved in the oneness of doing. We come to accept the wisdom of our actions when they are drawn from the well of synthesis that is the two-eyes dance.

Come dance, then, with Jumping Mouse, every day, every hour, every minute, giving away one eye to the buffalo and the other eye to the wolf; every instant of here and now screwing up our courage to leave Mouseland; every second blindly drinking from the waters of Medicine Lake; every second running safely beneath the broad back of the buffalo; every second cringing defenseless beneath the stooping eagle.

Jumping Mouse's New Name

Then he Woke Up. The surprise of being Alive was Great, but Now he could See! Everything was Blurry, but the Colors were Beautiful.

"I can see! I can See!" said Jumping Mouse over again and again.

A Blurry Shape Came toward Jumping Mouse. Jumping Mouse Squinted hard but the Shape Remained a Blur.

"Hello, Brother," a voice said. "Do you Want some Medicine?"

"Some Medicine for me?" asked Jumping Mouse. "Yes! Yes!"

"Then Crouch down as Low as you Can," the Voice said, 'and Jump as High as you Can."

Jumping Mouse did as he was Instructed. He Crouched as Low as he Could and Jumped! The Wind Caught him and Carried him Higher.

"Do not be Afraid," the Voice called to him. "Hang on to the Wind and Trust!"

Jumping Mouse did. He Closed his Eyes and Hung on to the Wind and it Carried him Higher and Higher. Jumping Mouse Opened his Eyes and they were Clear, and the Higher he Went the Clearer they Became. Jumping Mouse Saw his Old Friend upon a Lily Pad on the Beautiful Medicine Lake. It was the Frog.

"You have a New Name," called the Frog. "You are Eagle!"

The wolf had tricked Jumping Mouse. Actually, he had taken his other eye so that he could see. Death was clarity of sight. Wolf had led him to the very heart of the transforming vision. Into the sunrise of death Jumping Mouse ascended on trusting wings.

But is this the end of the story? Does the circle stop here? Eagle, formerly Jumping Mouse, rides high on the winds of illumination, piercing the veils that hang between his soaring spirit and the everlasting stars. With a sweep of his head he sees the Sacred River, roaring in the distance. Far off, he sees tiny dots scurrying to and fro, their little tails twitching, their whiskered noses up to the ground. Does Eagle remember that he used to live in Mouseland? The time will come when Eagle will give away one eye to Buffalo and the other eye to Wolf so that he can remember he is Mouse.

Jumping Mouse's quest for the Sacred River really had to do with learning how to jump. Unknown to him, he was practicing for the Big One, the one when he would hang on to the wind and fly. His journey to the Sacred River had been dying practice. It had helped him make all those other practice jumps on his way to the Sacred Mountains. And just when it seemed that his jumping practice was over, when he was blind as a bat, the Big One arrived. Why, it was that day at the Sacred River all over again. There was

Frog, sitting on a lily pad. And Brother Frog was saying the same thing he had said before: "Crouch down as Low as you Can . . . and Jump as High as you Can." Little Mouse was ready. He had been practicing his high jumping; he had learned how to die. But what did he see, as he rose on the wings of rebirth? He must have seen the Sacred Mountains shining in the distance.

This is where Raccoon came in. Remember? He told Mouse he knew what was causing the commotion in his ears. Mouse believed him and went down to the Sacred River with him. Raccoon left him there—or was it Mouse who left Raccoon? The days passed. Grandmother Nature smiled and frowned and enfolded him in her great arms. Through Frog she told him to jump as high as he was able. When he came back he had a new name—Jumping Mouse. Raccoon watched him return to Mouseland. He saw Jumping Mouse meet with misunderstanding and old habits. He watched the little fellow restlessly go to the edge of himself and with great courage run across the prairie toward the Sacred Mountains. He was so determined to perform the vision on earth for his people. But what about Raccoon? Where did he go?

The Jumping Mouse story does not offer a single clue as to the fate of Raccoon. One might surmise he continued to take other Mice down to the Sacred River to the source of the roaring in their ears. Apparently, Raccoon's life journey involves the gift of his eye to Mouse (the symbol of his people). This giveaway is what this book is all about.

But what does Raccoon gain from his giveaway-to-Mouse dance as he runs across the prairie to the foot of the Sacred Mountains? Can he expect any reward for his unflinching obedience to the roaring of the Sacred River? Will the Lord of the Sacred Mountains reward him with a turnip for his tummy? Will he be granted a higher step on the scale of incarnation? The real rewards lie in whatever he finds in Mouse's garbage can, things of benefit to himself and to the survival of his people. These things will shield him from the shadow spots of the prairie skies. If he works hard, is patient and tricky, his nose and sticky fingers will turn something up.

Of course, he who hears a roaring in his ears may not be Mouse. He may be Rat, Scorpion, Raven, Snake, Hawk, Deer, Cow, Road Runner, Spider, Fox, Worm, Rabbit, or Chuckwalla. Whoever he is, Raccoon will wind up learning about himself, and about the multitude of creatures of which his purpose circle is composed. He will discover how each one who hears the roaring is only a reflection of his own unique path across the prairie of his life. He will discover how he creates, and peoples, his world.

But really, who is Raccoon? That is one name for him, but does he have another, as Jumping Mouse did? Will he take the name of the shadow whisper that will ultimately fall on and transform him? Perhaps the best way to answer the question is to ask another: Who is Raccoon's greatest enemy—and ally? Of whom has he been most afraid all these years of running across the prairie?

Someday, like Jumping Mouse, Raccoon will reach the foot of the Sacred Mountains and give his other eye away to the wolf. There by the great Medicine Lake he will die alone and blind in his purpose circle. A large being will pounce on him like an explosion. He will go to sleep. Then he will hear a familiar voice calling to him: "Do you want some medicine?" "Yes! Yes!" Raccoon will eagerly reply. "Then crouch down as low as you can, and then stand up as high as you are able—and you will have your medicine."

Raccoon will crouch down and then stand up as high as he is able. Gradually, the darkness will fade. His eyes will open to the amplitude of space around him. Standing tall, looking down at his sturdy legs, he will realize that his upper limbs have been freed for a variety of tasks: gathering, shaping, sorting, planting, writing, organizing, hugging. As the birth mist clears he will sense the acuteness of his perceptions, the sweep and flow of his thoughts, the sharpness of his sensations, the tumult of his emotions, the steady love beat of his heart.

As he looks down into the mirror of Medicine Lake he will see his new body reflected. He will realize that he is both animal form and immaterial entity. Rooted to his feet of earth, his mind will reach beyond the cosmos and muse upon the existence of a Prime Mover. To the south he will hear the distant roaring of the Sacred River. To the west the sun will be setting over the great prairie of change and death. To the north the Sacred Mountains will loom, so near, yet so far. To the east, on the rim of dawn, the sun will ignite the wings of a soaring eagle.

"Is this really who I am?" he will remember, looking into the mirror of Medicine Lake, gladdened that he can see again.

"Do not be afraid of who you really are!" the voice of Nature will call to him. "Hang on to the earth and trust yourself to fly!"

Raccoon will grip the earth with his two roots and extend himself to the stars.

"You have a new name!" Mother Earth will call. "You are Human!"

Notes

INTRODUCTION

1. Hyemeyohsts, Storm, *Seven Arrows* (New York: Harper and Row, 1972).
2. Charles Bennett (1885–1930), "Philosophical Study of Mysticism," from *The Choice Is Always Ours*, ed. Phillips, Howes, and Nixon (New York: Richard R. Smith, 1951).

CHAPTER 1

1. Arnold Van Gennep, *The Rites of Passage* (Chicago: Chicago University Press, 1972).
2. Joseph Campbell, *The Hero With a Thousand Faces* (Princeton: Princeton University Press, 1970).
3. The three phases, *separation, marge, aggregation,* are invariably attributed to Van Gennep, 1972.
4. Cf. Mahdi, Foster, and Little, *Betwixt and Between: Patterns of Masculine and Feminine Initiation* (La Salle, Illinois: Open Court Press, 1987).
5. William Bridges, *Transitions: Making Sense of Life's Changes* (Reading, Massachusetts: Addison-Wesley, 1980).
6. A. P. Elkin, *The Australian Aborigine* (Sydney: Angus and Robertson, 1943).

CHAPTER 2

1. Mircea Eliade, *From Primitives to Zen* (New York: Harper and Row, 1967).
2. Physical plane dimensions of the ordeal are treated in Foster and Little, *Technical Guide to Threshold Safety* (Big Pine, California: Rites of Passage Press, 1987).
3. Jolande Jacobi, *The Psychology of C. G. Jung* (New Haven: Yale University Press, 1973).

CHAPTER 3

1. Joseph Epes Brown, *The Sacred Pipe: Black Elk's Account of the Seven Rites of the Oglala Sioux* (Norman, Oklahoma: University of Oklahoma Press, 1953).

2. Maria Leach, ed., *Standard Dictionary of Folklore, Mythology and Legend* (San Francisco: Harper and Row, 1972).
3. Cf. Victor Turner, *The Forest of Symbols* (Ithaca, New York: Cornell University Press, 1967).

CHAPTER 4

1. Campbell, 1970.
2. For detailed descriptions of a teacher's role during threshold emergencies, see Foster and Little, *A Technical Guide to Threshold Safety*, (Big Pine, California: Rites of Passage Press, 1987).
3. Foster and Little, *The Trail Ahead: A Course Book for Graduating Seniors* (Big Pine, California: Rites of Passage Press, 1983).
4. Bernardino de Sahagun, "Historia de las Cosas de la Nueva España," trans. H. B. Alexander, in *The World's Rim* (Lincoln, Nebraska: University of Nebraska Press, 1953).
5. Eliade, 1967.
6. Stephen Bacon, *The Conscious Use of Metaphor in Outward Bound* (Denver: Colorado Outward Bound, 1983).

CHAPTER 5

1. Martin Buber, *The Way of Man According to the Teachings of Hasidism* (Greenwich, Connecticut: Seabury Press, 1950).
2. Delores LaChapelle, *Earth Wisdom* (Los Angeles: Guild of Tutors Press, 1978).
3. Edmond Szekley, ed. and trans., *The Gospel of Peace of Jesus Christ by the Disciple John* (Berkeley: Shamballa Press, 1970).
4. Campbell, 1970.
5. Peter Balin, *The Flight of the Feathered Serpent* (Wilmot, Wisconsin: Arcana Publishing, 1978).
6. Storm, 1970.
7. Van Gennep, 1972.
8. Merwyn Garbarino, *Native American Heritage* (Boston: Little Brown and Co., 1976).
9. Marilyn Nagy, "Menstruation and Shamanism," in *Betwixt and Between: Patterns of Masculine and Feminine Initiation*, ed. Mahdi, Foster, and Little (La Salle, Illinois: Open Court, 1987).
10. Campbell, 1970.
11. Joseph Epes Brown, 1971.

CHAPTER 6

1. Joseph Epes Brown, 1971.
2. C. G. Jung, *Psyche and Symbol* (Garden City, New York: Doubleday, 1958).
3. Emphasized by Black Elk, in Brown, 1971.

4. Jerome Rothenberg, ed., *Technicians of the Sacred* (Garden City, New York: Doubleday, 1968).

CHAPTER 7
1. Bridges, 1980.
2. Cf. Brown, 1971; and Van Gennep, 1972.
3. Foster and Little, 1983.
4. Brown, 1971.
5. Manley Hall, *The Secret Teachings of All Ages* (San Francisco: The Philosophical Research Society, 1928).

221

Bibliography

Abbey, Edward. *Beyond the Wall.* New York: Henry Holt and Co., 1984.

Auden, W. H. *The English Auden.* New York: Random House, 1940.

Bacon, Stephen. *The Conscious Use of Metaphor in Outward Bound.* Denver: Colorado Outward Bound, 1983.

Balin, Peter. *The Flight of the Feathered Serpent.* Wilmot, Wisconsin: Arcana Publishing, 1978.

Blake, William. *The Complete Writings.* London: Oxford University Press, 1966.

Bly, Robert. *The Kabir Book.* Boston: Beacon Press, 1977.

Bridges, William. *Transitions: Making Sense of Life's Changes.* Reading, Massachusetts: Addison-Wesley, 1980.

Brown, Joseph Epes, comp. and ed. *The Sacred Pipe: Black Elk's Account of the Seven Rites of the Oglala Sioux.* Norman: University of Oklahoma Press, 1971.

Brown, Vinson. *Voices of the Earth and Sky.* Happy Camp, California: Naturegraph Publishers, 1974.

Buber, Martin. *The Way of Man According to the Teachings of Hasidism.* Greenwich, Connecticut: Seabury Press, 1950.

Campbell, Joseph. *The Hero With a Thousand Faces.* Bollingen Series, no. 17. Princeton: Princeton University Press, 1970.

Casteneda, Carlos. *Journey to Ixtlan.* New York: Simon and Schuster, 1972.

Chalmers, Lord, trans. *Further Dialogues with the Buddha.* London: Oxford University Press, 1926.

Chan, Wing-tsit, trans. and comp. *A Source Book in Chinese Philosophy.* Princeton: Princeton University Press, 1963.

Cirlot, J. E. *A Dictionary of Symbols.* 2d edition. Jack Sage, trans. New York: Philosophical Library, 1978.

Eaton, Evelyn. *The Snowy Earth Comes Gliding.* Spokane, Washington: Bear Tribe Publishing, 1981.

Eliade, Mircea. *From Primitives to Zen.* New York: Harper and Row, 1967.

———. *Rites and Symbols of Initiation.* New York: Harper and Row, 1958.

Eliot, T. S. *The Complete Poems and Plays.* New York: Harcourt, Brace and World, 1952.

Elkin, A. P. *The Australian Aborigine,* Sydney: Angus and Robertson, 1943.

Foster, Steven, and Meredith Little. *Technical Guide to Threshold Safety.* Big Pine, California: Rites of Passage Press, 1987.

———. *The Trail Ahead: A Course Book for Graduating Seniors.* Big Pine, California: Rites of Passage Press, 1983.

———. *A Wilderness Rite of Passage for Youth: A Teacher's Manual.* Big Pine, California: Rites of Passage Press, 1987.

Furst, Peter T., ed. *Flesh of the Gods.* New York: Henry Holt and Co., 1972.

Garbarino, Merwyn S. *Native American Heritage.* Boston: Little, Brown and Co., 1976.

Hall, Manley. *Secret Teachings of All Ages.* San Francisco: The Philosophical Research Society, 1928.

Harding, Esther. *Women's Mysteries.* New York: Harper and Row, 1976.

Harner, Michael. *The Way of the Shaman.* New York: Harper and Row, 1980.

Holy Bible, The. Authorized King James Version. New York: Oxford University Press, 1945.

Jacobi, Jolande. *The Psychology of C. G. Jung.* New Haven: Yale University Press, 1973.

Jung, C. G. *Psyche and Symbol.* Garden City: Doubleday and Sons, 1958.

La Chapelle, Delores. *Earth Wisdom.* Los Angeles: Guild of Tutors Press, 1978.

Lao Tzu. *The Book of Tao.* Frank MacHovec, trans. Mt. Vernon, New York: Peter Pauper Press, 1962.

Lucas, Crane, and Edwards, eds. *Grimm's Fairy Tales.* New York: Grosset and Dunlap, 1956.

Machado, Antonio. *Times Alone.* Robert Bly, trans. Middletown, Vermont: Wesleyan University Press, 1983.

Mahdi, Foster, and Little, eds. *Betwixt and Between: Patterns of Masculine and Feminine Initiation.* La Salle, Illinois: Open Court Press, 1987.

Mails, Thomas E. *Fools Crow.* New York: Avon Books, 1979.

Neruda, Pablo. *Neruda and Vallejo: Selected Poems.* Robert Bly, ed. and trans. Boston: Beacon Press, 1971.

Philips, Dorothy, ed. *The Choice is Always Ours.* New York: Richard R. Smith, 1951.

Roethke, Theodore. *The Collected Poems.* Garden City: Doubleday, 1962.

Rothenberg, Jerome, ed. *Technicians of the Sacred.* Garden City: Doubleday, 1968.

Rumi. *We Are Three.* Coleman Barks, trans. Athens, Georgia: Coleman Barks, 1987.

de Sahagun, Bernardino. "Historia de las Cosas de la Nueva España." Book III, appendix 1. In *The World's Rim,* H. B. Alexander, trans. Lincoln, Nebraska: University of Nebraska Press, 1953.

Snyder, Gary. *Regarding Wave.* New York: New Directions, 1970.

Sohl and Carr, eds. *The Gospel According to Zen.* New York: New American Library, 1970.

Squire, Charles. *Celtic Myth and Legend.* London: Dent and Sons, 1975.

Storm, Hyemeyohsts. *Seven Arrows.* New York: Harper and Row, 1972.

———. *Song of Heyoehkah.* New York: Harper and Row, 1981.

Strong, Emory. *Stone Age in the Great Basin.* Portland, Oregon: Binford and Mort, 1969.

Szekley, Edmond, ed. and trans. *The Gospel of Peace of Jesus Christ by the Disciple John.* Berkeley, California: Shamballa Press, 1970.

Torah, The. Philadelphia: Jewish Publication Society, 1962.

Turner, Victor. *The Forest of Symbols.* Ithaca, New York: Cornell University Press, 1967.

Van der Post, Laurens. *Heart of the Hunter.* New York: William Morrow and Co., 1964.

Van Gennep, Arnold. *The Rites of Passage.* Chicago: Chicago University Press, 1972.

Waters, Frank. *The Book of the Hopi.* New York: Random House, 1963.

Wilhelm, Richard, ed. and trans. *I Ching.* Princeton: Princeton University Press, 1950.

Wood, Nancy. *War Cry on a Prayer Feather.* Garden City: Doubleday, 1979.

Zaehner, R. C., ed. *Hindu Scriptures.* London: Dent and Sons, 1968.